'Muggeridge at his best, with Lord Reith, Cardinal Heenan, the Cistercian Monks, revisiting India . . .'

Birmingham Post

'An anthology of his broadcasts that is surely a unique tribute. It brings vividly back some hardly vanished memories and revives some scarce-healed regrets over things missed for ever.'

Catholic Herald

'How shrewd the interviewing is. And how free from malice. All the famous programmes are here – controversy, buffoonery, penetrating discussions with Bertrand Russell, Nye Bevan, Leonard Woolf . . .'

Manchester Evening News

'One of the most remarkable weavers of words in our times here speaks from the printed page with almost as much force and idiosyncrasy as when he appears on the screen. This vivid self-portrait is graced with some splended drawings by Trog.'

Church Times

Malcolm Muggeridge

Muggeridge through the Microphone

BBC RADIO AND TELEVISION

Edited by Christopher Ralling, With Drawings by Trog

COLLINS Fontana Books

First published by the British Broadcasting Corporation 1967
First issued in Fontana Books 1969

© *Malcolm Muggeridge 1966, 1967, 1969*

Printed in Great Britain
for the publishers, Wm. Collins Sons & Co. Ltd.,
14 St. James's Place, London, S.W.1.
by Richard Clay (The Chaucer Press) Ltd.,
Bungay, Suffolk

Contents

Contents

Contents

If, on the judgement day, I was confronted with God and I found that God took Himself seriously, I would ask to go to the other place.

Introduction

St Augustine, looking back in his Confessions on his time as a professor of rhetoric, scornfully described himself as a vendor of words. I, too, have earned my living by selling words, but prefer to call myself a communicator. In my earliest recollections I see myself holding forth to whoever would listen just for the delight of so doing, and I distinctly remember turning over the pages of books and newspapers when their contents were still largely mysterious. Already, it seems, the twentieth-century obsession with communication as an end rather than a means had taken hold of me. I was a disciple of Marshall McLuhan long before he had propounded his famous dictum that the medium is the message.

Thus radio, and later television, came to pass in my eyes as naturally and inevitably as sea navigation in the eyes of a Vasco da Gama, or internal combustion in the eyes of a Henry Ford. I saw nothing to marvel at in them; even now I find it difficult to think of them as having been deliberately invented. When mankind became possessed with a passion to move, lo! there was a wheel. Likewise, when they were possessed with a passion to communicate, lo! there were words. The wheel in due course became jet propulsion, supersonic flight, astronautics; the words were projected by rotary press, microphone, video-tape. Yet movement and communication remained the essential purpose. In other words, those two characteristic pursuits of our time – speed and mass-communications – are not to be regarded as something devised to make or mar our way of life. Rather, they are an emanation of it. If, as may well prove to be the case, they come to be seen historically as having brought about the destruction of our civilization, it will not be because of some malign impulse or force outside ourselves. We shall have done the job with our own hopes and desires – Prometheus tearing out his own entrails, gouging out his own eyes.

For me conscious communication began with print. What a moment that was in one's life when for the first time a limp, damp galley was laid on one's desk to be corrected, the ink running into little black rivulets as one attempted to write corrections on it! Empty words, no doubt, about some long forgotten issue, but read the next morning with such inordinate pride. Subsequently, there have been miles and miles of galleys, enough to encircle the globe; a preposterous paper-chase through the mists and swamps of troubled years.

I cannot pretend that my first acquaintance with broadcasting generated any comparable excitement. Written words, however evanescent, do briefly exist, like fireflies; spoken ones disappear as soon as they are uttered, carried away on the invisible waves of sound. Nowadays, of course, there is tape to preserve them, but only, surely, the most narcissistic or portentous temperament would incline one to listen to one's own past broadcasts. Even so, the broadcasting scene remains unforgettable – the airless, sultry studio; the little red light indicating that one is on the air; the flashing green light telling one to start or stop, to slow down or speed up; the inexorably moving hand of the noiseless clock; the figures behind the glass partition, so near and yet so remote; the glass of water always brackish to the taste; the sense of being far, far away from everyone and everything, in total isolation. How can I ever forget it?

The first broadcast I ever gave was on Sidney and Beatrice Webb. I have totally forgotten how I came to give it and what I said, but it must have caused offence because I received a letter from George Barnes – a bizarre but rather attractive ex-naval officer then bearing the extraordinary title of Director of the Spoken Word – briefly informing me that a scheduled repeat of the broadcast had been cancelled owing to objections which had been raised. This sort of thing, I have to confess, has quite often befallen me, though, believe it or not, in most cases I have been unaware, until it was pointed out, of the reason why. It is tempting to attribute such unawareness to a degree of innocence in oneself, or to an obsessive passion for the truth. A more likely explanation, I fear, is just a congenital awkwardness: a proneness to tread on people's toes and stumble against them, in deed and in comment. The punishment for me came – and there is always a punishment, and it is always appropriate – when, in the course of a broadcast, the producer held up a sheet of paper on which he had scrawled in large letters: 'Be controversial!'

Commander Barnes's admonition was followed by a lengthy lull in my budding career as a broadcaster, broken when I was invited to take part in *The Critics*, then young and in the spring. Incidentally, I expressed the opinion in those very early days of the programme that it could not possibly last, being too mannered, foolish, and altogether remote from the lives and interests of most listeners. Now, some two decades later, it is still going strong. When I was editor of *Punch* efforts were made to produce a parody of *The Critics* under the title of 'The Pundits', and for the purpose the scripts of past programmes were procured. Reading them through we realized that they defied parody; all we could hope to achieve would be just another *Critics* programme. The project was abandoned. This kind of thing is always liable to happen in bringing out a humorous magazine.

Being on *The Critics* involved going to a film and a play, reading a book, listening to a radio programme and visiting some sort of art show. It was one of those experiences which, though not particularly momentous in itself, yet stamps itself like stigmata upon one; the more so in my case because I have always had a rooted objection to being entertained or culturally uplifted. Having digested our pabulum, and having prepared one's own particular script – in my case, the book – one presented oneself at Broadcasting House on a Thursday in time for luncheon. Donald Boyd, an old colleague and friend of mine from *Manchester Guardian* days, presided. He has long ago retired, and I never see him, but vividly recall his brooding, ironic presence, conveying a sense – to me, most sympathetic – that human beings are always ridiculous, and never more so than when they clothe themselves in the magisterial garments of literary and artistic punditry.

Our deliberations began over luncheons (tasting, I used to reflect, of the Home Service), and received a certain amount of alcoholic stimulus. We each had an allotted role, mine being that of an ageing and already grizzled *enfant terrible*. It is the nature of mass-communications thus to require of their exponents that they should acquire and sustain a role, which in time takes over – poor Gilbert Harding for ever imprisoned in his irascibility, a Dimbleby in his pomposity, a Frost in his jocularity. We mass-communicators grow old and grey in the

service of our *doppelgängers*, and may expect, like Harding, at
last to succumb to them. There is no escape; if tonight I were to
recite the thirteenth chapter of Corinthians on the telly, viewers
would respond, according to their dispositions, by applauding
or denouncing my irreverence. 'They ever must believe a lie who
see with, not through, the eye,' Blake wrote. The microphone
and the camera are the greatest instruments so far produced for
hearing and seeing with, rather than through, ears and eyes, and
have generated, in consequence, a readiness to believe lies un-
equalled in human history.

After lunch we went upstairs to our studio and recorded the
programme. It was a talking marathon. Out of the babble of talk
occasional shrill cries would emerge, like the cries of sea birds
when waves are breaking on a solitary shore. I can still hear a
female voice shrilly proclaiming: 'I *liked* it!', and a male one in
a deeper key, but equally insistent: 'I *don't like* Raphael!' By
five o'clock we were finished, and emerged into Portland Place,
breathing in the air greedily after our incarceration; then, in my
case, on to Charing Cross and Fleet Street and, this time, a
typewriter, with a weight of dead words about my heart and a
sense of a lost afternoon, if not a lost life.

A similar scene was enacted for *The Brains Trust*, in which I
once or twice participated. It took place in the evening; the
meal was dinner instead of luncheon, and somehow, although
the food was the same, the occasion was more dignified and
substantial, perhaps because, in the mass-communicators' hierarchy, Brains take precedence over Critics. Whereas the latter
only traffic in opinions, the former are expected to dispense our
most sacred mystery – facts, the very sacraments of science. As a
Critic I proved inadequate, as a Brain non-existent.

When *The Brains Trust* was subsequently transferred to television I was for some weeks its chairman. We performed on
Sunday afternoons, after lunching together at Scott's in Picca-
dilly, and driving out to the fastnesses of Shepherd's Bush in a
large Rolls-Royce which, as I learnt from the chauffeur, was
normally used for funerals. Our set was supposed to convey a
book-lined study with an open fireplace and a blazing fire. The
books were mostly dummies, with a few bound volumes of
sermons and Victorian poets which, for purposes of verisi-
militude, could be detached; the blazing fire was electrically

operated, with sham logs. On one memorable occasion John
Betjeman seized one of these and waved it in the air to illustrate
some point he was making about contemporary architecture.

A more popular and, to me, congenial version of the same
procedure is *Any Questions?*, put out by the BBC's West Re-
gion, and, like *The Critics* and *The Archers*, a marvel of
longevity. The audiences, I observe, are visibly growing older, as
also, of course, are we, the performers; the Baroness Stocks and
Freddie Grisewood (the esteemed chairman) were not born
yesterday, no more was I. Shall we, perhaps, one day all drop
dead to the question, put by a lady from Stroud in the studio
audience, as to whether the panel would like to live for ever?

The studio audience, incidentally, on radio and television,
deserves a special study by some student of politics, if not by
Robert McKenzie. Watching it react, as I so often have, to
instructions, in sign language or held up on a board, to laugh,
applaud, groan, sob or yell, it has seemed to me a perfect image
of twentieth-century universal-suffrage-democracy. One man
one vote, one audience one laugh – so runs the road from Social
to People's Democracy; from Locke to Lenin; from 1789 to
1984.

Television, as far as I was concerned, came like a thief in the
night. I cannot pretend that I saw its great potentialities.
Almost overnight one was suddenly aware of the glassy eyes of
television sets staring vacantly at one across sitting-rooms, of
aerials rising like dreaming spires into the city, of cameras
silently closing in on one, of a microphone just too far away
from one's mouth for a bite to be taken at it. Thenceforth the
bulk of the citizenry were to be preoccupied, not with life itself,
but with the image of life in a little screen; meeting there the
great ones of the earth, watching there the contemporary scene,
imagining that they have climbed in there themselves. Television
has proved a great venture in collective narcissism – nature held
up to a mirror instead of the other way round; all the stage a
world.

It was Andrew Miller-Jones, the founding-father of *Panorama*, who first asked me to appear on television. I was to go out
to Harringay where one of Billy Graham's meetings was being
filmed, and afterwards to have a studio conversation with him.
At Harringay for the first time I saw the cameras in operation.

Subsequently, of course, I became all too familiar with that strange little procession, consisting of cameramen, sound recordist and their acolytes, all wired together as with an umbilical cord, moving concertedly, almost conspiratorially, hooded gun-microphone held aloft, their tread deliberate and restrained like a spirited horse on a snaffle. Likewise that other telly-scene – two chairs in a studio, arc-lamps overhead, cameras advancing upon one and then retreating, their little red lights glowing, making them seem bloodshot-eyed, and the floor-manager, battery at his belt, ear-phoned, raising an admonitory finger, dramatically dropped in a signal to begin.

I heard myself asking Billy Graham questions, and him answering them. It ought to have been strange, seated there together under the arc-lamps, but actually it wasn't. Everything that happens on television takes place outside oneself; there is a telly-world apart, in which one can watch and listen to oneself in complete detachment. Encounters in this telly-world might take place in outerspace for all the impression they make. I must, I suppose, have met on television at one time or another most of the eminent and the notorious figures of the day – from Bertrand Russell to Harold Wilson, from Salvador Dali to Lord Fisher of Lambeth, from Jawaharlal Nehru to Norman Mailer and six anonymous Black Muslims. Practically the only one who made any lasting impact was Brendan Behan, and that because he was too drunk to be able to utter at all, so that I had to conduct the interview with myself, both putting and answering the questions. Alcohol had immunized Behan to the telly-virus; it did not take. Though speechless, he remainned his authentic self, and we met in the flesh instead of ethereally, on the TV screen. I was glad to learn subsequently that our encounter benefited him. West-End managers who had been chary of his plays queued up for options on them after he had been seen drunk on the telly.

After the Billy Graham interview I appeared fairly regularly on *Panorama*. Practically everything was done live in the big studio at Lime Grove. The various items were set up, and we all assembled in our corners for transmission. Thus there might be in one corner a brass-hat with a map and a pointer ready to explain something or other, in another a bus-driver to talk about traffic congestion, and I in yet another with a famous surgeon who had lately separated a pair of Siamese twins. I particularly remember this surgeon because, when we went on the air, I disgraced myself by being unable to think of anything better to ask him than whether, supposing they wanted it, he would be able to join the twins up again.

It was after I had been appearing on *Panorama* for rather more than a year that I first saw myself described, in an article in the *Sunday Express,* as a television personality – a distasteful epithet at the best of times, and in that setting abhorrent. The article featured a large blow-up of my face with the caption: 'The Face You've Got to Look at For the Next Two years.' Up to the appearance of this article I had never been conscious of attracting undue attention as I went about my lawful occasions – at that time, editing *Punch.* Thenceforth I began to be aware of people staring at me. Did they stare because I now expected them to? Or had they been staring all along without my noticing? In any case, television *is* being stared at. One offers oneself for show, and can scarcely complain if one attracts attention, off as well as on the screen. Such fame or notoriety is peculiar to our time. In the past if someone was famous or notorious, it was for something – as a writer or an actor or a criminal; for some talent or distinction or abomination. Today one is famous for being famous. People who come up to one in the street or in public places to claim recognition nearly always say: 'I've seen you on the telly!' It is very rare indeed for them to recall anything one has said, and even when they do they more often than not get it wrong. They are the viewers, one is the viewed.

Thenceforth appearing on television was to be a part of my life. I cannot pretend that this has been a source of unmitigated satisfaction, or, for that matter, of unmitigated dissatisfaction. My feelings remain mixed. There is something, to me, intrinsically unsatisfactory about the medium, but this may well be due simply to my years. Television, on the producing side at any rate, is for the young, who have the requisite enthusiasm and energy, and who therefore dominate it. In the television Centre I often feel, and no doubt look, like a white-haired vicar dropping in on a teenage rock-and-roll session in the church hall. The medium, as it seems to me, requires so much and yields so little. All the hours one's spent filming, in cutting-rooms, in dubbing studios; and then, hey presto! – some fleeting minutes on the screen, and all's gone for ever. I believe I never once walked off a set without a feeling of at any rate partial failure; a desolate sense that what had been achieved was miserably incommensurate with what had been envisaged.

Naturally the programmes I took to most easily were those which approximated most closely to straight journalism. Thus my part in *The Thirties* – a compilation of newsreel material of the period brilliantly assembled by Therese Denny – was really a writing job. Similarly with two other programmes we made on the rise of American and Soviet power in the twentieth century, which went out as *The Titans*, my part was, essentially, to write the commentary.

Also in the vein of journalism were television documentaries, upon which I ventured under the pleasant and stimulating auspices of Alasdair Milne. He sent me to India with Kevin Billington to recapture times I'd spent there forty years before when, as a young man fresh from Cambridge, I'd gone to Travancore (now Kerala) to teach at a Christian college. The resultant programme – *Twilight of Empire* – is the one which, of all the programmes I've been concerned in, gave me most satisfaction. Encouraged by the interest in this fragment of telly-autobiography, I had a go at a programme about my formative years, also directed with great skill by Kevin Billington – *A Socialist Childhood*.

Another documentary – this time with Jack Gold – that I much enjoyed was based on an American lecture-tour I undertook. The programme, when it appeared, was considered by some to have presented too unkind a picture of certain of the lecturing occasions and audiences, and I was criticized for having ridiculed those I was paid to address. On this basis, Swift would have been debarred from ridiculing the Anglican Church, Voltaire from ridiculing Frederick the Great, and Evelyn Waugh from ridiculing Fleet Street and press lords – which, as Euclid says, is absurd. After the lecture-tour I stayed on in America with Michael Tuchner to do the filming for a programme I'd long meditated – *The American Way of Sex*. There was, heaven knows, no shortage of material, and selecting and editing it gave, I'm afraid, a lot of trouble. Nor was the final result seen on the screen by any means satisfactory, though I impenitently take pride in it, if only because it tried to say something which, in my opinion, much needed saying: that the erotic obsessions of our western way of life are calculated to destroy love, happiness, and ultimately sex itself, not to mention sanity.

It was Grace Wyndham-Goldie who produced the idea (and who has been more productive in thinking up good ideas for television programmes than she?) for a series of programmes called *Let Me Speak*, in which I would talk with groups of young people with something emphatic to say. We began with young Jesuits, worked through young Marxists, Humanists, League of Empire Loyalists, Moral Rearmers, Anarchists and Ursuline Nuns, and ended up with John Birchites and Black Muslims. It was a strenuous, but I think rewarding, enterprise. I liked it if only because it was, by its nature, concerned with minorities, all too often ignored in these days of worship of the consensus – that false god.

Latterly especially I have found myself increasingly pre-occupied with the exposition on television of religious questions. Is this even possible? I am by no means certain. If the founder of the Christian religion had been provided with broadcasting facilities, would His words have touched more hearts sooner? It does not follow. As it was, spoken to little obscure gatherings of mostly illiterate people in a remote part of the Roman Empire, they were to ring through the world for two thousand years. The waves of sound and light might have carried them further more quickly, but in the process what they gained in speed and coverage could easily have been lost in inspiration and author-ity. Who can tell? In any case religious programmes have been decreed, and interest in religion increases, not diminishes, with the decay of religious belief, in the same sort of way that the sick grow ever more conscious of their bodies. In a documentary about Lourdes, *Pilgrims to Lourdes*, directed by Michael Tuch-ner, I tried to convey something of the poignancy and miracu-lous cheerfulness of the sick who gathered at St Bernadette's shrine, and in another, *The Road to Canterbury*, directed by Therese Denny, to give some impression of the sort of religious questioning that is going on inside people today. The latter was open to the criticism of being too discursive and vague to arrive at any firm conclusions – apart, I should add, from the only two among those questioned who had a firm faith, a doctor and a nun. Yet it may be that this very inconclusiveness appealed to

viewers who recognized in it their own case. I have noticed over
the years a growing disparity between the judgements on television programmes of professional critics and experts and those
of viewers. In television, as in literature and the arts, a man-
darin class had been produced whose attitudes, judgements and
very language diverge ever more widely from the commonalty.
Another religious programme which gave me particular pleasure
and satisfaction was *A Hard Bed to Lie on*, directed by Lawrence Gordon Clark. We took the cameras inside an enclosed
Cistercian Abbey at Nunraw, and produced, as I hope, a true
picture of the monks and their way of life.

Now that Dimbleby is dead, I suppose that I look back on a
longer more or less continuous span of television appearances
than any other extant performer. Nearly all of it has been under
BBC auspices, though there was a period of estrangement when
I fled to the bosom of Mr Sidney Bernstein, and another when,
along with Ludovic Kennedy, Robert Kee and some other
tellymen, an attempt was made to go into independent television
production. It ended, I may add, disastrously, if not ignomini-
ously; certainly hilariously.

My relations with the BBC have been like a marriage, with
ups and downs, infidelities on both sides, and separations, but
miraculously we remain together, I suppose because, in a sort of
way, we suit each other. During the years of our associations the
Corporation's whole character and standards have undergone a
drastic change, due, at any rate partially, to the competition of a
commercial channel, and the consequent pursuit of high rat-
ings. When John Reith shaped the BBC into a paternalistic
public corporation, to be a monopoly, as far as he was concerned, for ever, he saw it as Christian in outlook, orthodoxly
authoritarian in cultural matters, and, if politically neutral, as
essentially as the Church of England a part of what is now
called the Establishment. The structure withstood his departure
for a number of years, but in time there were rumblings, and
finally a break. It came in the shape of the now famous programme, *That Was the Week that Was*, directed by Ned
Sherrin, which satirized in the most cheeky and usually amusing manner everything and everyone without respect of principles or persons. Thenceforth all taboos and restrictions were
broken, until now, short of showing the act of fornication on

the television screen (this may well come, at any rate on BBC 2), it is difficult to see what remains unsaid and undone. This process of liberation was exhilarating, though its appeal with each successive version – *Not So much A Programme, BBC 3, The Late Show* – inevitably diminished. Satire lives by its comedy and dies by its smut; when the former is in short supply, the dosage of the latter tends to be increased, with calamitous results.

By a curious irony the BBC, famous for its propriety, began to err in matters of taste as only the respectable can when they decide to be improper, whereas ITV, which had been expected to he heinously vulgar, leant over backwards to preserve the properties. How strange a reversal of roles! – Auntie kicking up her heels in the most indecorous manner, and Mr Lew Grade insistent that nothing should be said or done on the screen which, in the words of Mr Podsnap, would bring a blush to the cheek of a young person. How, from my point of view, even stranger that I should find myself discussing these matters before the television screen in the course of marathon dialogue with Lord Reith himself! Yet so it happened.

The sound and video tapes and film of all these programmes will, for the most part, have long ago been very properly disposed of; the scripts remain, a high, forbidding pile, and it is

from them that this volume is taken. Thumbing it gingerly over, I ask myself what, if anything, I have been communicating, and like Pilate do not wait for an answer. I even wonder whether, properly speaking, I have been a communicator at all. Readers, as I hope, will be able to judge for themselves. The selection, I should add, was made largely by Christopher Ralling, whose idea this book was and to whose enterprise its appearance is due. If it deserved a dedication it should be to him and to Tony Kingsford of BBC Publications, who put it together and supervised its publication.

Ireland

Ireland is so poor, its population is declining, they're so indolent and generally scatty, that there's no possibility of the twentieth century being set up there. And that's the place I have in mind to retire to.

Computers

You can leave two computers in a room by themselves without the slightest anxiety.

An Interview with Myself

QUESTION: Mr Muggeridge, how far have you deliberately set about becoming a provocative or controversial figure with a view to attracting notice?

ANSWER: It's terrifically difficult to be completely honest in a matter of this kind. In all sorts of public presentations of oneself there's bound to be an element of showing off; something vulgar has always been recognized in being a public personage in any degree, and this is no doubt why the finest minds and the most sensitive spirits have preferred to live retired, if not monastic, existences. At the same time I think I can say with honesty that I have not sought to disagree; it's merely that ever since I began to look at the world at all, I can remember having a sort of odd view of it, as though the things that were going on, on the public stage, had nothing to do with me, and therefore seemed simply bizarre and ridiculous, subjects for ridicule. That perhaps is the source of one's reputation, such as it is, for being provocative or controversial.

QUESTION: Take, for instance, the views you've expressed about the Monarchy. Are they genuinely held or just an exercise in showing?

ANSWER: Oh yes, the views that I've actually expressed about the Monarchy are genuinely held, but of course if you touch on a matter like that, which for a variety of reasons is a sort of raw nerve in society, what you actually say tends to get completely lost in the stirring up of public prejudice. My own genuine view is that the Monarchy is not a thing that matters very much. I think that, as it stands at present, it's a tremendous focus of absurdity, because it's an institution which is unrelated to our true circumstance. I never really said any more than that, or cared any more than that about it.

QUESTION: You are always denigrating people, running things down. Why are you so negative in all your attitudes?

ANSWER: What does negative mean? We've got a notion today that people must be optimistic, that people must think every-

thing's going to turn out well. This is a very new and quite fallacious view of life. I think it is utterly ridiculous for an individual to think that through his appetites, living as a mortal man on this earth, he can be happy. Just as I think it's utterly ridiculous to imagine that any society of human beings, however well organized, however affluent the circumstances, could produce a collective happiness. If however I've taken a negative view tactically, strategically I've always assumed, and feel more than ever as I grow older, an intense optimism. In other words it seems to me that life is good, and that in some mysterious way the experience of living can only be of benefit to the individual and to all life of which he's a part. Exactly how this is, of course, one doesn't understand, but in that sense I feel completely positive in attitude, but utterly negative and impenitently negative about man's prospects in terms purely of his earthly existence.

QUESTION: Is there no one you admire?

ANSWER: Oh many people, many people, but when that question is put it nearly always means, Is there no one in power, no one famous, no one eminent, no one rich, no one distinguished whom you admire? Of course many, many human beings, the great majority of human beings with whom one is thrown into contact, are delightful people, towards whom one can feel without any hypocrisy or forcing a sentiment of love. But it is true that power and the desire for power, the appetite for power and all the things that go with power, the desire to be eminent, to be admired, do bring out the basest side of human beings, and that those in authority always have been, are now, and always will be, the most despicable of human beings, and as such deserving of ridicule and non-admiration.

QUESTION: So negative, critical and pessimistic a view of contemporary circumstances would seem to make for unhappiness. Are you unhappy?

ANSWER: Not at all. On the contrary, as I get older I find myself happier and happier. Happy first of all about the earth itself which seems to me ever more beautiful each year as I watch the cycle of the seasons. About my fellow-humans: those whom I know intimately and those with whom I come into casual contact seem to me ever more marvellous, so that happiness grows; but notice this is a happiness which only exists because it is unrelated to material and sensual satisfaction.

QUESTION: You always seem to be talking and writing about religion. Is this like a hypochondriac talking about health, because you haven't got any?

ANSWER: That depends what you mean really by religion. I certainly find that the dogmas of the religious faith to which we all belong, and on which our civilization and way of life is based, namely the Christian religion – that these dogmas are to me completely incredible. I can't possibly and could never believe in them. But if religion means seeing that life consists of more than its phenomena, that it has a meaning which must be in transcendental terms, then I can say with perfect truth and sincerity that I am religious. I know without any shadow of doubt that the Christian religion is correct when it tells men and women that if they seek to satisfy themselves solely with what their flesh and the world offer they die in spirit. And if they want to live in the spirit, it can only be by seeing that happiness lies elsewhere than in earthly things.

A Socialist Childhood

A fragment of autobiography

At the age of three months I was awarded a prize for being a plump baby – the only prize I ever received for anything. After this distinction my first clear memory is of my father and his cronies plotting the overthrow of the capitalist system in the drawing-room of our suburban house in South Croydon. They were, I suppose, odd conspirators – all very respectable citizens but, in my childhood eyes, men of destiny. Everything that mattered to me in those days took place in that room. There the conspirators gathered on a Saturday evening – round the fire or, when the sun was shining, by the open French windows – looking out in the garden, fortifying themselves with mild libations of Scotch and water. My mother dozed in her chair, and I did my best to efface myself, for fear of being noticed and sent to bed.

As they talked I seemed to hear a revolutionary mob, myself in the vanguard, making an assault on the Croydon Town Hall, and the sound of the tumbrils rolling along Birdhurst Gardens, as they carried the Mayor and Corporation to the guillotine. Like the early Christians waiting for the end of the world, we waited for the end of the capitalist system, which, as I confidently believed, would be largely brought about as a result of the efforts of my father and his cronies.

My father habitually left the house in the morning round about eight o'clock to go to the City, having gulped down his breakfast. I would post myself at the front garden gate to make sure of being able to accompany him to East Croydon station. As we walked along he would dilate upon the impending collapse of the capitalist system. In my mind's eye all its then citadels – banks, shops, tall factory chimneys – collapsed and fell, as though stricken in some mighty earthquake. And in their place a new, virtuous socialist Croydon arose. Not so, it would appear. This new Croydon which has arisen is neither socialist nor noticeably virtuous.

Already Croydon's office workers were rolling city-wards. Croydon East to London Bridge via Penge. It was like a blood-stream, red corpuscles swarming through the arteries of commerce, trickling into the network of little veins to nourish the muscle, the tissue, the nerves of the relentless city. My father hated his work as a ledger-clerk in a City counting house. In his eyes, he was helping to sustain the system he so longed to destroy. His real life began when the blood-stream flowed back to Croydon East, to be enriched again for the next day's course. I was waiting, anxiously on the look-out for him; with infinite relief spotted him coming up the ramp, always in the forefront – a small bearded man striding along vigorously. In those days he was everything to me; the centre of my universe.

More often than not my father went straight to the Town Hall from the station. On rare occasions I was permitted to sit in the public gallery to watch the Borough Council proceedings. The mayor presided, and spread out before him were the Aldermen and Councillors, my father among them – in those days the solitary Socialist. They seemed a majestic body, though even then a vague sense of the absurdity of authority and its trappings began to afflict me. From the public gallery I looked down enthralled, feeling myself to be in touch with the established social order itself. This was its very citadel, and my father had breached it; in him the Council had admitted to its deliberations its own destroyer. How I hung on his words when he rose to defend the virtuous trams against the villainous private enterprise buses! With what withering scorn he denounced the niggardly ratepayers' representatives whose only concern was to keep down public spending. Later my father became a Member of Parliament, but it was in Croydon rather than in Westminster that I saw him most vividly as a Socialist David pitted against the Capitalist Goliath. With his agile mind for a sling and devastating words for pebbles he would, I knew, lay them all low.

Some of my father's fellow-Socialists found his patient, Fabian, municipal tactics too slow and pedestrian for their taste. They travelled further afield, bicycling – ladies daringly in bloomers, men in Norfolk suits – as far as Gloucestershire, to found a colony at Whiteway. This was to be their Arcadia.

Though none of them had ever put spade to earth except to plant a geranium or bed out a lettuce, they easily saw themselves planting and reaping the golden corn they needed; providing for all their simple wants with their own toil; building their homesteads. Money, marriage and other ills were to be abolished, and happiness, based on brotherly co-operation, to prevail. Today the homesteads are in poor shape. Money, it seems, refused to be abolished, marriage reared its ugly head, brotherly love yielded to unbrotherly quarrelling. This kingdom of heaven on earth, like so many before it, failed to materialize.

Among other eccentric practices, the colonists were in the habit of bathing in the nude in a stream which ran through their land. This interesting spectacle provided me with biological instruction by the direct method. I gazed curiously at the unclothed bodies of the matrons, and with rapture at their slimmer more shapely daughters. It would surely have astonished the colonists to know, when they first came to Whiteway, that their last resting place was to be a country churchyard. After all their revolutionary purposes what a conventional and English outcome! I expect too that the then Rector would also have been astonished to know that his domain was to accommodate them throughout eternity. In life he looked askance at their sandals and their socialism, at their free unions and occasional nudity. In death they became acceptable. The English social scene has a way of absorbing everything at last – even rebellion. In any case, my education continued elsewhere.

My first school was what they then called a Board School; the local recreation ground my childhood pleasure garden, where my adolescent dreams first burgeoned. Here I first fell in love. The excitement of a school badge suddenly seen, the enchantment of fair hair falling under a round felt hat ... and a dogeared dictionary with her name on the fly-leaf – Dora P., Upper Fifth.

August 1914 broke into everybody's recreation ground, even a schoolboy's. I was by this time at the local borough secondary school, subsequently transformed into the Selhurst Grammar School. If Waterloo was won on the playing fields of Eton, the class war was assuredly lost on the asphalt playgrounds of secondary schools like mine.

HEADMASTER: Mr Muggeridge has come to talk to you this morning, and you will know that he is an old boy of the school. Mr Muggeridge.

MUGGERIDGE (addressing the class): School in my day was a place to get away from as soon as possible and for as long as possible. Everything exciting, mysterious, adventurous, happened outside its confines, not within them. My days have not been haunted by any lingering adoration of some God-like athlete, compared with which adult fleshly love seemed coarse and obscene. Our adolescent sensuality was directed exclusively towards girls, whose persons, as we grew older, we ventured to explore in scented cinema darkness, or beside blackberry bushes in the August sun. Our South London cockney grated on the ear. Despite prefects' colours and other trappings reminiscent of Tom Brown's Schooldays we were irretrievably urchins of the suburbs. When I embarked upon the arduous but infinitely exhilarating pursuit of the meaning of things, it was from the bottom of a stony hillside, with no golden memories of lost innocence about my heart. No one ever seems to forget Eton, I easily forgot my borough Secondary School.

Cambridge is a romantic dream in the minds of those who didn't go there. It was more a realization of my father's ambitions than of mine. To him the University symbolized all he felt he had missed in life: the magical and mysterious grace which he had seemed to see in his Fabian heroes and heroines. Now on his behalf I was to join the company of the golden youths. Always I have felt in this world something of a stranger in a strange land; but never more so than in my undergraduate days. The very air seemed heavy with tedium and boredom. The sleepy dons drained their subjects of life and interest, their falsetto facetiousness even more painful than their prosy banalities. Proletarian boys tend to succumb to Cambridge's allure. Instead of manning the barricades, they hang around in the corridors of power, join the Garrick Club, take to bathing in the morning, and dining in the evening. I found no joy in any of the University's life. It had the rank stench of a decaying class in a society which was itself in the last stages of decomposition. I took my sombre and often solitary rides to Grantchester, indifferent as to whether or not there was honey for tea, or whether the church clock had stopped at ten to three.

This sense of isolation was exaggerated by the fact that the great majority of my fellow-undergraduates had been at public schools. I did not understand their slang, play their games or share their ways. It was my first acquaintance with the upper classes and I did not like them. In my day faint derivatives of Rupert Brooke were still around, all too self-consciously unprepared for the long littleness of life, toasts of homosexual dons, pale youthful bodies, lithely swimming in Byron's pool. Already, as I saw it, the sun was setting on this golden world. It was a dream I failed to share, and, after four non-productive and undistinguished years, I gladly contracted out to spend the next six in Egypt and India. After which I became a journalist and, at the age of 26, was washed up on a desolate shore indeed – the *Manchester Guardian* in the depression.

The Industrial Revolution, leaving desolation along its trail, was now moribund. Lancashire, in the early thirties, was an outward and visible manifestation of the downfall of capitalism, as my father and his cronies had predicted in our South Croydon sitting-room. I exulted to think that everything was coming to pass under my very eyes just as they had envisaged.

On the *Guardian* we worked to the famous C. P. Scott, an old Liberal cock valiantly crowing in a neglected farmyard where weeds grew unchecked and the stench of decay rose in the air. The hopeful views we expounded on his behalf seemed to me increasingly remote from the circumstances which actually confronted us. We were looking not outwardly at the world, but inwardly at a reflection of our enlightened selves.

It has always seemed to me ever since I can remember that the only human achievement that mattered was to write. Words written and spoken were all. I envisaged many immortal works, all unwritten, and even managed to produce a few most mortal ones. I suppose when I come to die the strongest impression of life will be a sheet of white paper on a desk or in a typewriter which needs to be filled. We leader writers were posted each in his separate perch along what was called the Corridor. Nightly we typed out our editorial exhortations – the voice of Liberalism, righteous and enlightened; putting the world to rights, telling our fellows the way that they should go, championing the downtrodden and oppressed. We believed, not entirely without reason, that our words went ringing round the world. It is so no longer. The present editor of *The Guardian* sits, not in C. P. Scott's seat, but in London. The famous *Manchester Guardian* has become *The Guardian* merely. The lights that burnt so brightly in Cross Street are growing dim. The voice is muted that spoke so confidently and so eloquently. Here in its very cradle the Liberal mind reaches its last decrepitude – becoming a civilization's death wish.

By now I was married. Sharing my life with my wife Kitty, having our four children, has been one of those experiences that so transcends others, as well as the accompanying emotional and sensual wear and tear, that in the end there is nothing to say about it. But however she looked at it, marrying Kitty – a niece of Mrs Sidney Webb, and with other eminent social connections, was a leg-up socially. The Webbs, in relation to the hierarchy of the Left, were Ducal. From the point of view of a career – that dread word – things looked good.

In due course the Webbs, like the Whiteway Colonists, were accorded an appropriate resting place – in their case in Westminster Abbey along with the Captains and the Kings. Before this blessed consummation I, as a nephew-in-law, enjoyed their gracious favour. My father – dear man – readily stomached Mrs Webb's somewhat condescending attitude to the connection. I was not so pleased. The *Guardian*'s liberal inanities were ever more sour in my mouth. The economic depression hung over my spirits as it did over Lancashire. Increasingly Communism loomed up as the way of salvation, and Moscow as its heavenly City. I pined to be gone there. 'In Russia, Sidney and I are icons now,' Mrs Webb said to me once, striding through Hampshire shrubland, her dog Sandy and her consort Sidney panting along beside her. By the time they came to die the Webbs were icons here too.

It was from the Webb's warm Fabian nest that I took off for Moscow in the autumn of 1932. They sped me on my way, clucking sympathetically. There was, as I then believed, this other paradise to go to, and thither I duly went.

Keir Hardie

I've attended a great many Labour Party conferences, sitting in the reporters' gallery, and we always used to exchange a look up there when anybody got up and said 'If Keir Hardie were alive today', because we always knew we were going to hear some even greater boloney than the normal speeches. My own opinion, for what it's worth, is that if Keir Hardie *were* alive today he would be an eager and active member of the Right Wing of the Conservative Party.

Is the Notion of Progress an Illusion?

A conversation with Bertrand Russell

MUGGERIDGE: My position is this – I consider that one of the major factors in reducing the world to its present rather melancholy condition has been the circumstance that human beings have been conditioned, for a variety of reasons, to believing that in some extraordinary way human life must, or can, get better and better. Now I regard this as a complete fallacy. I don't think it gets better, nor, indeed, do I think it gets worse. And I think that the only way that human beings can live sanely in this world is by recognizing that, and therefore I contend that the idea of progress has been a disintegrating idea, a fundamental error, and that there's very little hope for us until it's ultimately exploded.

RUSSELL: Well, if one accepted the view that nothing that anybody can do will make the world either better or worse, one might just as well take to drink and sink into the gutter. And it seems to me that it's not the view that you really take, and you don't really believe it.

MUGGERIDGE: I must utterly disagree with that, because I don't think that not believing in progress – believing as, for instance, Christians have always believed, that human life is inherently imperfect, and that it cannot be other than imperfect, because they are imperfect – I don't believe that that has produced a sort of enervation. There's absolutely no reason why people shouldn't become richer, why they shouldn't invent things, why they shouldn't make their lives more comfortable. All that's got no bearing on the particular question that we're discussing. What we're discussing is whether human life itself is progressing, is getting finer, richer, better. In my opinion, not.

RUSSELL: There are, you admit, changes in our circumstances. What you do not admit is that those changes are either for the better or for the worse? You've maintained that they're ethically neutral, and if you hold that, honestly and sincerely, it does follow that it doesn't matter what you do at all, and that all ethical standards – all ethical and moral standards are at an end.

MUGGERIDGE: Not in the least. I'm not at all saying that changes in human life don't matter. I'm saying that they don't alter its essential character, and that if people attribute to them qualities that in fact they don't have, they are pursuing a fallacy, and ultimately wreck their lives. In other words, it may or may not be desirable that you should have things like radio, this strange invention that is enabling us tonight to be heard by other people. It may or may not be an advantage that that exists, but it has no bearing on this idea of progress. On whether you and I are better people, more likely to understand the circumstances of our existence.

RUSSELL: I don't think one ought to confine oneself to scientific discoveries. Now, there have been savage societies in which, when a man got old, his children sold him to neighbouring cannibals, to be eaten, and I think you and I would agree that that was a bad system, and we prefer the system in which old men are allowed to go on.

MUGGERIDGE: I should have said, myself, that if you added up the appalling cruelty of the time we've lived through, both collective and individual, it would create a world record, and I believe that there's some connection between that and this extraordinary illusion that human beings are progressing. Because I think that what really makes human beings humane and kind is humility, and the idea of progress is an arrogant idea. And that is probably its greatest moral disadvantage.

RUSSELL: I think that we've got to get down to a certain point. Are we thinking of better or worse only in moral terms or also in other terms. Now, if you're thinking only in moral terms, then I think there's a great deal to be said for your attitude, but I should say that a community is better, for example, in which people are healthy than one in which they are ill, although that's nothing to do with virtue.

MUGGERIDGE: Then you would look for the best human beings – for the highest human achievement in those communities which had most successfully mastered the problem of their material existence, and if you did that, you would be bitterly disappointed. I'm thinking for instance of someone like Gandhi who, though in many ways a very pig-headed man, had in my opinion a very profound idea, and his idea was that this assumption that by industrializing India, for instance, by making India richer, you would necessarily make it a better place was wrong. You may say that his whole movement was an anachronistic movement, but I think it contained a very great truth, and this is precisely the truth that I'm trying to get at in this proposition.

RUSSELL: Well, I think that that implies extraordinary limitations of human sympathy. The poverty of India was such that most children died in infancy, and if they survived they survived in conditions which were extraordinarily painful. If you had human feeling, if you had love in your heart, if you felt that you cared whether people suffered or not, you wouldn't like that; you would only like it if you put spiritual values, which you enjoy and the other fellow doesn't, above material well-being, which is very important when you get below a certain level.

MUGGERIDGE: I think that everything in the whole story of mankind which is great has come from a pursuit, however foolish and obscurantist, of spiritual values, and that everything that's base and everything that's common and everything that's cheap has come through the pursuit of material values. I want to ask you, Lord Russell, to take two human beings, extreme cases. Let's take a man like St Francis of Assissi, and let's take a man like Henry Ford. Now both these men perfectly genuinely believed that they were serving their fellows, and I consider that St Francis of Assissi's contribution to the business of human life was infinitely greater than Henry Ford's.

RUSSELL: I should deny that *in toto*, and I don't think you recall what happened to the Franciscan movement as soon as he died. As soon as he died the Franciscan order turned themselves into recruiting sergeants for one of the most bloody wars in history. That was the effect that he had in the long run. Ford hasn't done anything like that. Ford was far more spiritual than St Francis of Assissi.

MUGGERIDGE: I would say that what progress really means, as I see it, is the creation of a kingdom of Heaven on earth, of perfect conditions on earth, and I believe that to be complete boloney, a complete fallacy. Whereas the other idea is the idea of

human beings who can conceive a kingdom of Heaven in Heaven, a much finer, more wonderful, more productive idea than the idea of a kingdom of Heaven on earth which was Ford's idea.

RUSSELL: Where I fundamentally disagree is that I think the really important thing is that people should have compassion and sympathy – that they should mind when other people suffer. You can't be content with these spiritual values which consist of ignoring the rest of the world.

MUGGERIDGE: Of course, those spiritual values are really the only things that ever have made human beings have compassion.

RUSSELL: I should deny it – all through history I should say that people who have concentrated on spiritual values have produced hell. I think the Nazis concentrated on spiritual values.

MUGGERIDGE: Dear Lord Russell! Of all people they most believed in material values – they most believed in progress and, my goodness, what a show they created! They utterly believed it, they were tremendously progressive.

RUSSELL: If you see vast masses of populations suffering appallingly you must look for some means of diminishing their suffering.

MUGGERIDGE: Are we to understand that you don't believe in progress?

RUSSELL: You're not to understand that I foretell that there will be progress. I don't know whether there will or not. I hope there will be.

MUGGERIDGE: And what would you regard as progress?

RUSSELL: Well, I should regard it as progress if the average person was happier than he had been.

MUGGERIDGE: So would I.

RUSSELL: Now look, it's all very fine, this talk, but the majority of mankind at present are suffering from under-nourishment. Getting enough to eat is material and if you don't get enough to eat, you suffer, and I will not say that on account of spiritual values I'm content that the majority of mankind should go hungry.

MUGGERIDGE: Nor am I, nor am I. I hate the idea of any single human being being hungry; what I am interested in is how you create in our fellow-men a desire that those who are hungry should be fed, and that one man should not be cruel and brutal to another; and I believe in so far that it has been done on earth, it has been done not through this idea that man can live by bread alone, but by the idea that he can't and that when you absolutely understand that he can't live by bread alone, you in fact are much more likely to give him bread than if you say he can. You see, if you are right, these immensely successful materialist societies of our day would be places of love and happiness, and in fact they're not.

RUSSELL: I didn't say they were places of love, but I do think that undoubtedly the average inhabitant of the United States is happier than the average inhabitant of India at the present day.

MUGGERIDGE: And better?

RUSSELL: There you come back to morals. I don't want to go into morals because I think morals are controversial.

MUGGERIDGE: We must be controversial, we can't divorce this from morals. It's an impossible thing to do. What I actually believe, if you want to know, is that basically there is only one thing that makes human beings seek one another's good and that is expressed in the religious concept of love; that that alone mitigates the horror of competing and hating mankind.

RUSSELL: Now may I answer that. If you study the history of religions, you will find that they have been incredibly full of hate, of persecution, of intolerance, that they have been among the main reasons why human beings have inflicted suffering upon each other, and in proportion as religious belief has decayed, people have grown more humane.

MUGGERIDGE: I have lived in two societies where religion was systematically destroyed. One was the Third Reich, Hitler's Germany, and the other was the USSR – Russia, and in those two countries I have seen more cruelty, more callousness, than anywhere else I have ever been.

RUSSELL: That is because both of them were inculcating a new religion. They both had a religion and a new one, and new religions are more intolerant than old ones, and it was the religious intolerance that made them be so cruel and so bad.

MUGGERIDGE: I think the only thing that any human being could possibly seek to achieve is to be good.

RUSSELL: Oh good heavens, I'd cut my throat if my motive in

life was to be good. I mean it seems to me the most priggish and horrible object to have in your life.

MUGGERIDGE: I think it's the only one.

RUSSELL: And if you wish to be good you're not forgetting self.

MUGGERIDGE: Of course you are.

RUSSELL: People who wish to be good are just horrible to my mind; and are completely defeating the end, they'll never be good, never, never...

MUGGERIDGE: It comes down ultimately to what it means to be good. Now you say this is an abhorrent idea.

RUSSELL: I said it was abhorrent to make it your motive in life to be good, which is quite a different thing.

MUGGERIDGE: But that is the very fount of Christianity.

RUSSELL: And one of my objections to Christianity.

MUGGERIDGE: You think it's a horrible religion. It's also true of every single religion that's ever been. So they're all horrible.

RUSSELL: All, yes.

MUGGERIDGE: All horrible.

RUSSELL: Yes.

MUGGERIDGE: Then you would wish that not one of them had ever existed.

RUSSELL: I should. Now look here, when the question of euthanasia was discussed in the House of Lords, a bill was brought in to legalize euthanasia, and all the noble Lords who were Christians got up and said (I paraphrase their remarks) that God sends cancer to people because He likes torturing them; and you balk Him of His pleasure if you allow them to commit suicide.

MUGGERIDGE: Well they were foolish men to say that.

RUSSELL: They were Christians, and all the Christians said that.

MUGGERIDGE: Well, I would have voted against euthanasia, because I accept the fact that life is benevolently intended; and that therefore I would never take the responsibility of saying that I, a human being, can decide to bring the life of another human being to an end.

RUSSELL: But look here –

MUGGERIDGE: Because I – I am not sufficiently arrogant to be able to say that.

RUSSELL: Look here, Muggeridge. If you say that an omnipotent creator has created this world out of benevolence, you have to go through such incredible contortions –

MUGGERIDGE: But I don't –

RUSSELL: – that you can't emerge a whole human being.

MUGGERIDGE: I can see that it's quite conceivable that there are things in life which seem to me to be abhorrent and awful, but that in relation to the totality of the experience of living, both in time and beyond time, they would be comprehensible.

RUSSELL: Let me put you the opposite hypothesis, which is just as plausible. There are, we admit, some good things in the world. The world was created by Satan, who put these good things in the world because they increased the evil of the bad things; and that would have fitted the facts just as well.

MUGGERIDGE: But I just don't happen to believe it.

RUSSELL: No, because it doesn't suit you, it's uncomfortable, no other reason except comfort.

MUGGERIDGE: Not at all, because it would in many ways be much more comfortable to take quite a different view. But everything that I've seen of life and read about life and everything I've admired in life points to the conclusion that it is in fact benevolently intended.

RUSSELL: I see. So when Giordano Bruno was burnt alive, he was tenth-rate and vulgar and the people who burnt him were great?

MUGGERIDGE: No.

RUSSELL: But that's implied in what you said.

MUGGERIDGE: It isn't at all. I think the fact that he would be burnt over a matter of belief entirely ministers to what I believe. The fact he would do it. The fact that he would think it worthwhile to be burnt, rather than assent to something which, if life were as trivial as a materialist philosophy would suggest, would have meant nothing.

RUSSELL: But why should a materialist philosophy suggest that life is trivial? It doesn't suggest any such thing.

MUGGERIDGE: It does to me.

RUSSELL: It does to you because you don't understand it.

MUGGERIDGE: Maybe that's it.

RUSSELL: I'm being very nasty, forgive me ...

MUGGERIDGE: No you're not ...

RUSSELL: Yes I am, I'm being horrid.
MUGGERIDGE: You're not being horrid at all.
RUSSELL: I've been intolerant...
MUGGERIDGE: You haven't been intolerant.

Belief

I don't believe in the Resurrection of Christ, I don't believe that
He was the Son of God in the Christian sense, I don't believe
that He was born of a virgin. But I consider and, every day that
goes by, see more clearly that what Christianity has taught, the
view of life, and I don't mean any twopenny ha'penny thing like
ethics, I mean a profound view of life – statements like 'if a man
would save his life he must lose it', things like that – I see in
them not only a profound truth, but a glowing truth, so that the
perception of them is more than agreement. You could regard it
as a mystical experience.

Ladies and Gentlemen, it is my pleasure

Reflections on an American Lecture Tour

The day has come round again. From every corner of the globe we, the L men, are converging on New York. The American lecture season is about to open. Ladies in Eau Claire Wisconsin await my coming. Santa Maria California, do not lose heart – I'll be with you soon. Jewish ladies in Los Angeles – Executives in Seattle – Art lovers in Chicago – I'm on my way.

The American appetite to be addressed is inexhaustible. From us a message; from them a dollar. Hungry sheep look up and are, one hopes, duly fed. A lecture tour is perpetual motion. In trains, in aeroplanes, in motor-cars, one's ancient carcass is relentlessly transported to and fro, and up and down, America. At Gettysburg this weird odyssey begins. Ah – if only it was possible to be as brief as Lincoln!

America is largely made of cardboard, which at night shines and blinks with deceptive neon, wonderful to behold. If only, as G. K. Chesterton remarked, one couldn't read. Endlessly repeated exhortations to eat, to drink, to sleep, perchance to dream. Banners of a vast consumer's army bravely held aloft. 'Onward affluent soldiers, marching as to war, with the "national product" going on before.' Such is the approach to every American city. Ahead, emerging like mountain peaks, the central core of skyscrapers.

The thing Americans most like doing, I always think, is driving a big car along one of their highways – mile after mile, hour after hour. No means of knowing where you are; not in a sense going through the country at all – going through nothingness, as though the motion itself produces a sense of restfulness.

Not long ago I was driving across this country from coast to coast, and arrived at a small town, a tiny American town, late at night. And I saw four neon signs standing out in the darkness. One of these signs said 'gas', one said 'beauty', one said 'food', and one said 'drugs', and with a feeling of absolute exultation I realized that these were the four pillars of the modern world. This was the American way of life. A super-abundance of gas, and food, and beauty, and drugs.

Americans often seem like a looting army. They, as it were, invade and occupy their own country, gorging their own provisions, sacking their own cities, grabbing their own treasure, raping their own women. Will they perhaps in the end repulse the invading hordes – themselves – winning a glorious victory in self-destruction?

Advertising

If you are going to advertise it's almost certain that you'll exaggerate, and therefore ninety per cent of advertising is lies.

In America particularly, some of the best brains, the best endeavour in the country is being devoted solely to persuading people to want what they don't want, to get rid of things before they're worn out, to buy other things that are totally unnecessary, and it's only by all that activity that this mad society can run.

Mini-mania

There's nothing in this world more instinctively abhorrent to me than finding myself in agreement with my fellow-humans.

The American Way of Sex

Sex is the mysticism of materialism and the only possible religion in a materialistic society. In America today the religion of sex has reached its highest point of development and attracted the largest number of adherents. The devout dedicate their lives to sex, from the cradle to the grave and even beyond. The sacred pornographic texts, from *Kama Sutra* to *Fanny Hill, Chatterley*, the *Cancers* and *Candy*, edify the faithful. As do film goddesses, seen through a camera lens brightly, black or white or in glorious technicolor. Eat this, wear this, anoint yourself with this, in remembrance of sex. Even the cadavers are perfumed and pomaded in case there should be a chance for a tumble in the coffin and dating through eternity. Rarely if ever in history has a religion attracted adherents so zealous and so numerous. It is of sex that cherubim and seraphim continually do sing. In the beginning was the Flesh, and the Flesh became Word. In the spoken and the written word, in neon signs, on rotary presses, on the waves of sound and light that overflow the ether, the new evangel is joyously proclaimed – to die in the spirit and be reborn in the flesh.

Sex sells anything from deodorants to bulldozers. It's the magic ingredient, the packaged thrill, the plastic glow. Oh, vestal virgins of Madison Avenue. Oh, Aphrodite, rising so fragrantly, so exquisitely out of the mist of universal desire. Even the dolls must have reached puberty to be interesting. The bra precedes the breast.

To the outward eye, a campus in Ohio presents an idyllic scene. There the young co-eds bound as to the tabor's sound. Where in the wide world would you find such artlessness combined with such earnestness? The sorority houses are aviaries where the singing birds try out their fledgling wings. Freed now from parental control, still liable to be strict in these Middle-Western regions, these are the nurseries, the learner slopes in the great pursuit of happiness on which Americans, and following them mankind, are bent. Blithely and innocently prepared for

the long littleness of sex, with youth at the steering-wheel, and pleasure in the rear seat, they're all agog. On their heads, just and unjust, the erotic persuasion of advertisers, pundits and pornographers falls like black atomic rain.

Each separate elegant home, each lush convertible is a temple dedicated to the cult of sex, to the assiduous practice of *erotica domestica*. Sex is pleasure, marriage is virtue, and ever the twain shall meet. Marriage is a Grecian urn whose lovers, though they may not be outwardly for ever young, must engage in transports that are for ever fresh. Many willing hands and minds assist them. Nor need the coming of the menopause, the passage of years, the decay of the body, the dropping out of hair and teeth, abate their ardour. Let me not to the marriage of true bodies admit impediment. In sickness and in health, till death them do part, they may continue to pursue happiness in one another's arms. Oh, sex, where is thy sting?

If I were a woman, I'd rather be a whore than a bunny.

Pilgrims to Lourdes

A journey with the sick

The departure platform has a different air from the others. The departing are pilgrims, many of them sick. For them travelling presents particular difficulties. They are not holiday-makers in the ordinary sense. They are bound not for a beach or a resort, but for a shrine – Saint Bernadette's, the most popular Christian cult of modern times. The sick and the crippled make the arduous journey in the hope of a miracle. The others who are whole and well help with the disabled, and look to receive spiritual edification themselves. I find so outrageous a defiance of the twin contemporary gods of science and pleasure very much to my taste.

On this train the sick are the centre of attention – not shunned as they tend to be in our humanitarian societies, where they remind us of the fallibility of all human endeavours. Thinking about it, it's an extraordinary thing that in the middle of the twentieth century there should be this great load of people, some sick and some well, some old and some young, hoping to some degree, consciously or unconsciously, for a miracle. I thought that travelling with so many sick people, and some of them very sick, would be depressing. Actually it's not. There's a terrific atmosphere of an outing. And of course when you think about it, quite apart from any hopes of being made physically better, if you spend your days in a hospital bed, or incapacitated, a trip to Lourdes, on any showing, is a lift to the spirits. One dreads to sentimentalize men and women so afflicted. I need not have worried. They are easy to talk to, and disarm mawkish pity by their robust attitude to their misfortunes.

MAN WITH CRUTCHES: I'm suffering from disseminated sclerosis, it's a brain disease sort of thing, which affects the walking and movements of the legs.

MUGGERIDGE: Makes it more difficult to get around?

MAN: Yes, I can't get around without sticks and I go very slowly.

MUGGERIDGE: And you're hoping at Lourdes to throw those sticks away?

MAN: I'm hoping to wrap them around somebody's neck.

MUGGERIDGE: I give you full permission to wrap them around my neck. If you don't get a miracle will you still have been glad to come?

MAN: I will indeed because I think it's very spiritually refreshing.

MUGGERIDGE: What's that mean?

MAN: Well, refreshing from the point of view of the hereafter sort of thing.

Rolling across the plains of France the pilgrims have their rosaries, their prayers, their offices, and their friends and helpers to sustain and solace them. Whether hopes of heaven are well- or ill-founded I do not know; but certainly they help to make earthly misfortunes more bearable.

MUGGERIDGE: Tell us why you are going to Lourdes.

PILGRIM ON TRAIN: Well I'm going to Lourdes primarily because I believe strongly that it is possible for a miracle to occur, not necessarily to me but to someone in the pilgrimage some time. But if it doesn't, it doesn't make any difference at all – one is strengthened spiritually, and even physically in a sense, because one is able to go on with one's life as it is. And you get a renewal of strength.

MUGGERIDGE: This happened to you when you went before?

PILGRIM: Yes, I found a great improvement. In fact before this present pilgrimage my mother remarked that she found an improvement in me, generally, after being at Lourdes. I was very much worse than I am now, but I did improve physically.

MUGGERIDGE: Have you always been bedridden like this?

PILGRIM: Yes, from birth.

MUGGERIDGE: Do you think a miracle might happen to you?

PILGRIM: Well, I think it is possible. Not necessarily to me but to someone. It could happen to me with the mercy of God. I really believe that God is almighty, and that is not just a figure of speech, but in fact He is almighty.

I was never before on quite such a journey as this one, now nearing its destination. So harrowing, and yet so cheerful. What a waste of time, effort and expense, it might be urged, to transport these unfortunates so far; and yet, looked at in another way, how infinitely worthwhile for them and all concerned.

The pilgrims' destination is the Domain within the town of Lourdes, where the cult of Bernadette is practised. It's devised almost like a stage set. At all times and seasons pilgrims come in tens of thousands, of all races, nationalities and classes, but mostly poor and humble, to pray, join processions, meditate, and, as they hope, to commune with their saint. The place is never still, and never empty; drama is endlessly enacted – of blessings and mercies ardently beseeched, and of misfortunes and disappointments meekly endured. One has to come to the grotto where Bernadette is reputed to have had her vision either very early in the morning, or very late at night, to find it other than crowded. At those times it really does, in some mysterious way, give one a sense of being in a holy place, if only because of the millions and millions of people who come and worship here, in all seasons and all times. Even on a rainy morning there is a crowd of worshippers clustered round the grotto. What, I ask myself, brings them there? I should say hope, hope of better health, for a stronger faith, for their soul's salvation maybe, or for more trivial mundane things – like easier circumstances, and fulfilled ambition. Not only, or even particularly, for themselves but for those they love. It's easy to ridicule acceptance of the magical qualities of this place and of the waters of the spring people drink and bathe in. One can look with a sceptical eye at the rather unconvincing display of crutches allegedly cast aside by cripples who've been miraculously cured. I find no such inclination myself. It seems to me in all sincerity, and even humility, that these Lourdes pilgrims – mostly very humble lowly people – may have had a clearer and even more practical vision than other traffikers in hope in our time, like psychiatrists and advertisers, and travellers to the moon.

The grotto where Bernadette is reputed to have had her vision is, of course, above all where the pilgrims want to be.

They go there eagerly and leave reluctantly: ravaged, patient faces endlessly passing. Who dare say that they should be deprived of this so precarious hope in favour of another, ostensibly better founded, in the shape of a coloured capsule, a sharp knife, some human disentangling of their human ills? Certainly not I. The water from the grotto, eagerly swallowed, medically speaking, probably does as much, or as little, good as any other medicine.

Although the Lourdes weather is notoriously changeable – close and overcast, and unsuitable for the sick – the pilgrims cheerfully take their meals, whenever possible, in the open air.

MUGGERIDGE: Doctor, I imagine that you would have to select, to some extent, people who could undertake a journey like this?

DOCTOR: Yes, we do have a regular series of selection committees, and they have to get very special certificates from their own doctors, telling us about the disease, and as to whether they are really fit to travel.

MUGGERIDGE: Of course, in a way to say they weren't fit to travel would be in itself a sort of contradiction of the thing.

DOCTOR: Yes, of course a lot of people do try to swing it – they do get away with murder – but we are prepared to take people who are pretty well near dying. We have facilities for taking stretcher cases, and in actual fact, as it turns out every now and then, one, perhaps two, even one year three people died here. They come on those conditions really. If they're dying, it's their lot anyway. They're most of them pretty ill. There's only one end to their illness, unless they're cured unexpectedly.

MUGGERIDGE: Are they – I mean, would it be true to say that the majority of cases here are from a medical point of view hopeless cases?

DOCTOR: I should think so, certainly eighty per pent of them are – they've been ill for – usually many years. They're not going to get better unless something unexpected happens.

MUGGERIDGE: And this something unexpected means a miracle?

DOCTOR: Yes, that's in the theological sense. In the medical sense of course we don't talk of miracles, we talk of 'inexplicable cures' – cures that are not explainable by natural means.

MUGGERIDGE: Have you yourself witnessed a miracle?

DOCTOR: No. Miracles are few and far between.

MUGGERIDGE: What happens – I mean in your opinion as a doctor – what happens when one of these miracles takes place?

DOCTOR: Well the sort of miracles that happen at Lourdes are usually normal cures, with one unexplained factor, and that is that they occur instantaneously.

MUGGERIDGE: Doctor, one last point I'd very much like to put to you is whether there's any real point in protracting the life of people in such a sorry state as they are. What do you feel about that as a doctor?

DOCTOR: Well, we've had people coming here year after year. I've one man in mind: gradually from coming in a chair he was brought on a stretcher; and he gradually curled up and the only sign of intelligence in him was a twinkle in his eye. He had to be fed, he had to have everything done for him, he could just swallow. And he'd look at you and make a sort of ugly leer, but when you saw him, when you saw his whole face, you realized how beautiful his smile was, and poor old Jock, he lived a full life right to the very end.

Particular importance is attached to bathing in the waters of the grotto. Outside the baths the pilgrims wait their turn for a dip. It is a very ancient notion that bodily and spiritually imperfections may be washed away like dirt in clear water. I think of the Ganges at Benares black with bathers; of the leper who emerged from bathing with his flesh cured and wholesome. Willing hands, to the accompaniment of intoned prayers, dip battered bodies into the water from Bernadette's spring. Magic? Superstition? Sublime faith? Something of all three I expect. At any rate, for the battered bodies at least some refreshment, one hopes.

In Lourdes it goes without saying that the Roman Catholic Church is present all the time. The streets throng with monks and nuns and ecclesiastics of varying orders and degrees. The air is full of the sound of prayers being intoned, and of hymns and anthems being sung. In the Middle Ages I suppose it would all have seemed natural enough, but to a twentieth-century mind, bruised and battered by the ferocious currents of our time, it seems more disconcerting and even alarming. Though I hasten to add that the music is magnificently evocative and like the prayers still conveys, as was originally intended, the longing for perfection of hearts intrinsically imperfect. In such circumstances it's natural, as it were, to stand apart and look at this ancient faith moving in so dramatically opposite a direction to the pursuit of happiness in terms of affluence and sensual satisfaction on which the bulk of mankind today seem to be so ardently bent. Is it a dying echo of a splendid but now abolished past? Or does it still enshrine the only valid answer to the confusions and conflicts of an age like ours, one of the cruellest of history, and at the same time, materially speaking, one of the most fabulously successful? I have to admit that I personally alternate from one view to the other. But this I can truthfully say: the pilgrims who come to Lourdes do seem to derive from the offices of the Church a spiritual strength to face their misfortunes with fortitude and even at times exultation. Stretched out in their wheelchairs and their stretchers, to await a blessing that won't cure their stricken flesh – they still have quite a festive air, compared with psychiatric wards, where the children of affluence rage and fret.

Each afternoon a procession forms. For the sick, wheeled into position in front of the Basilica, this is the day's awesome moment, when, if at all, their anguished prayers will be answered. It is infinitely touching to see mothers carefully manoeuvring their children into position to be as near as possible to the Host when it passes. This, of all times, is when a miracle might happen. Perhaps today ... perhaps today some desperate and humanly incurable malady will pass; an inhuman look be made human; God's handiwork restored. Perhaps today....

MUGGERIDGE: I was thinking, when I watched you going round in the procession, that there were those people stretched out, and they hear the words from the priest 'God can cure you', and I thought perhaps if I'd been lying there, being an impatient and worldly sort of person, I should think, Well, why doesn't He?

BISHOP: Why doesn't God cure all the sick in the world? Surely this is to infringe on God's domain and to plan people's lives as we would wish them planned, not as He would wish them planned. And none of us can say that we share in divine wisdom to that extent, can we? We are very proud of our planning, we plan the political and social issues of this world. Do they always turn out to be wise plans? Isn't it absolutely necessary for us to try to conform our minds with the mind of God, to try and see His designs, His plans? If a person is not cured physically, it doesn't follow that that sick person hasn't a very definite purpose in life.

Bernadette is looked to for help – touching her rock, like touching a loving face, beseechingly. It is a rock like any other rock geologically speaking; the water under scientific analysis indubitably H_2O. Yet not to the pilgrims. To them a rock of ages cleft for them; the water a rare and precious balm of great worth. Lourdes itself is as dedicated to the pilgrims as Stratford-upon-Avon is to Shakespeare. Some find the souvenirs offered for sale in such numbers repugnant. They are not very appealing, but I dare say inevitable. In any case, they don't appear to trouble the pilgrims, who for the most part are too poor to be other than meagre purchasers.

To most people Lourdes signifies the sick and the dying, and they do, it must be said, loom large in this place. Sometimes one sees them with a certain disquiet and even distaste, as extras brought on and off the stage in a macabre way, in the presentation of a Christian morality play. At other times, their cheerful fortitude seems a particular glory, and puts to shame one's own complaining about ills so incomparably less exacting. The question inevitably poses itself as to whether these maimed, stunted lives should be protracted, and, in the case of congenital defects, ever begun. Can these poor souls, one asks oneself, sometimes in outward appearance barely human, really wish to go on living? The scientific answer, of course, is emphatically no. In a broiler house, there's no place for such poor specimens. They are, to use a particularly odious expression, useless mouths. But then, our world is not a broiler house, though alas, as we've seen, it can easily be made one. If the Christian view is correct, and mankind is a family, with a Father in Heaven who can't see even a sparrow fall to the ground without concern, then these twisted, tangled bodies have as rightful a place in the human family as any others, even when they can scarcely utter their insistence that life has been to them a precious gift, and they duly offer thanks to their Maker for it. I, as it happens, believe them more readily than I do the pronouncements of experts on population and eugenics. It can be argued, it seems to me, that no lives are worth living, or that all lives are worth living, but not that some lives are worth living and others not.

In the torchlight procession the little candles separately carried make one pattern to the accompaniment of one melody. The faces pass like shadows, and I watched them pass, envious perhaps of their serenity, and of the certainty which shines in their candles. So many hearts which might legitimately be uplifted, with their ever ardent endlessly repeated 'Ave Marias'.

Such is Lourdes. With the pilgrimage over the pilgrims return, little if at all better in body, but surely heartened and strengthened to face a continuance of that other unremitting pilgrimage – their daily lives.

An Eighth Deadly Sin

One of the peculiar sins of the twentieth century which we've developed to a very high level is the sin of credulity. It has been said that when human beings stop believing in God they believe in nothing. The truth is much worse; they believe in anything.

Hymns

I think that hymns are very underrated things, that some of the most exquisite melodies of modern times are hymns; they may well in the future be as precious to people as border ballads were.

Air Hostesses

If a woman is pretty and she smiles at me I want to be sure, or my vanity wants to be sure, that she's smiling at me to please

me, and if I see a girl smiling at everybody with equal idiot amiability it's irritating.

Virgin Birth

It would have been attractive on many occasions in one's rather murky past if one could have put forward this theory with assurance.

Lord Reith Looks Back

John Reith, first Director-General of the BBC, was born in Scotland in 1889. Youngest son of the Minister of the College Church, Glasgow, he was brought up in the strict religious atmosphere of the Manse. On leaving school he served an apprenticeship as a locomotive engineer. He joined up on the outbreak of the First World War, and, as a lieutenant, was severely wounded in France in 1915.

In 1922 he joined the BBC as General Manager. After shaping and directing it for fifteen years he resigned, hoping that he would be called upon to play a significant role in the conduct of the war he knew was coming. He became Chairman of Imperial Airways, and a few months later he formed BOAC as a public Corporation and was its first Chairman. In the early years of the war was successively Minister of Information, Minister of Transport and the first Minister of Works, under Chamberlain and then Churchill. Subsequently he joined the RNVR, becoming Director of Combined Operations Material – a department of the Admiralty which, charateristically, he invented himself, and which played an important part in the D-Day landings. He was knighted in 1927 and created Baron Reith of Stonehaven in 1940.

The Early Years

MUGGERIDGE: Were you a bright student?

REITH: No.

MUGGERIDGE: But you were interested in your studies, weren't you?

REITH: I was interested, but I had no stimulus to excel. I got through examinations too easily.

MUGGERIDGE: Games?

REITH: Rugby in particular, rugby football. After some years I was moved from forward to take the place of the full back who'd been hurt. I never moved from the full back position.

MUGGERIDGE: That suited you.

REITH: That suited me. Can you see something in that?

MUGGERIDGE: I can see that as a forward you were one of a pack, and you couldn't really stand up in a pack too much. As a back you would put up an individual performance.

REITH: Absolutely, and one was on an establishment of one's own, so to speak.

MUGGERIDGE: I've read that you used to go walking when you were young, in the dark with the wind blowing, and that's where you felt yourself to be isolated?

REITH: Yes, I was trying to determine what I was meant to do in the world, feeling that I was meant to do something, not just to be a mediocrity.

MUGGERIDGE: But why isolated? That's what I don't understand.

REITH: You mean lonely?

MUGGERIDGE: Lonely.

REITH: Yes, very lonely.

MUGGERIDGE: Without friends, without intimates?

REITH: Very, very few friends indeed.

MUGGERIDGE: Now why was that?

REITH: Possibly I wasn't a friendly character myself.

MUGGERIDGE: Or perhaps this feeling of having some tremendous destiny of your own?

REITH: Maybe. Bit arrogant, isn't it?

MUGGERIDGE: I don't know. It's a thing that some men have had, this feeling. When you write about it, it's as though the wind had so much to do with your thoughts.

REITH: Ah yes, particularly when it came nor-westerly or northerly.

MUGGERIDGE: Now why should that be?

REITH: From Ben Lomond and the hills running at the beginning of the Grampian Range. I used to think, you know, particularly when there was a wind and a sound of music in the trees, that there was a message for me, but I couldn't quite make it out. Couldn't quite make it out.

MUGGERIDGE: Never caught it.

REITH: Never caught it.

REITH: A real job, and on one's own.

MUGGERIDGE: But I still can't quite see what was going on in your head.

REITH: A struggle to find guidance, guidance from my own self I suppose, if I couldn't get it from the others, as to what one was to do.

MUGGERIDGE: Were you tremendously ambitious?

REITH: I was tremendously over-serious, I think. I doubt if I've ever been young. I don't think I took the potential enjoyment of life as most people of my age would and did.

MUGGERIDGE: Because you were too serious?

REITH: Yes and inordinately ambitious, I suppose, to be fully stretched, which is a word I've been asked to explain before, to be fully stretched; inordinately ambitious to be of real service.

MUGGERIDGE: Ambition must have been directed into certain concrete forms, mustn't it? You must have wanted to be this or that.

REITH: No. Because, deplorably, I couldn't make up my mind as to what I wanted to do. I left school with a vague feeling that I wanted to go to Oxford or Cambridge for Classics. You know what Robert Louis Stevenson said about engineering? The most arduous form of idleness. Nobody can talk to me about hours of work or about care in turning out a job. Getting up at a quarter to five in the morning, a fifty-six-hour week and quite often overtime. And three-hour evening classes almost every night.

MUGGERIDGE: It's fascinating for me to speculate if you'd gone to Oxford instead of Glasgow, because I loathe Oxford myself.

REITH: Well switch over to Cambridge.

MUGGERIDGE: I hate that even more. I feel that if you'd gone and been subjected to that very insidious kind of brain-washing that these older universities go in for, you wouldn't have been this man that you are, and I think much less.

REITH: I hear you.

MUGGERIDGE: Going back –

REITH: Did you get what I said just now?

MUGGERIDGE: You said, I hear you.

REITH: That's a Scots expression.

MUGGERIDGE: What does it signify?

REITH: I hear you – that the remark is not worth answering or that the remark that had been made was untrue. You never heard that?

MUGGERIDGE: I never heard it. Would you say that you had, when you were a student, a fairly clear set of values that you had accepted and that therefore dominated the way you looked at life and the way you thought of living?

REITH: Yes.

MUGGERIDGE: If you had to say in a few words what it is, what would you say it was?

REITH: A passionate desire for truth in oneself, one's actions, in one's believing. And kindness.

MUGGERIDGE: Meaning sympathy, understanding in dealing with other human beings. What's called love.

REITH: I haven't used that word love. I have particularly avoided using that word.

MUGGERIDGE: Why?

REITH: Because it's awfully misused. You know the lines from Burns –

> If we had'na loved so kindly,
> If we had'na loved so blindly,
> Never met, nor ever parted,
> We had ne'er been broken hearted.

That's one kind of love, isn't it?

MUGGERIDGE: Yes. Marvellous. Do you have such regrets in your own life?

REITH: If you want to follow up and embarrass me more, you will say, 'Were you thinking of a particular individual?'

MUGGERIDGE: Well, I do say it.

REITH: And if I said no, you wouldn't believe me.

MUGGERIDGE: I wouldn't.

REITH: Well then, I don't say anything.

MUGGERIDGE: You've got to say yes.

REITH: I've got the last word.

MUGGERIDGE: That's a brilliant evasion, because I can't proceed any further. But of course the truth is that I don't think anybody could live to be your age or mine without some experiences which those lines would in some way convey. Isn't that true?

REITH: I hear you.

The BBC

MUGGERIDGE: When you saw that famous advertisement for a General Manager of the British Broadcasting Company and you went into that place in Kingsway, did something tell you that this was the end of the quest?

REITH: Before that. It was very odd. One evening in Regent Square Presbyterian Church the Minister, Dr Ivor Roberton, preached a sermon about the Lord requiring a man to fill up a gap, and he said, 'Maybe there's somebody in this congregation tonight that might be called to fill a considerable gap.' Extraordinary thing. . . . And this entry in my diary finished the day, 'I still believe there is some great work for me to do in the world,' And I found the BBC, or the BBC found me.

MUGGERIDGE: Tell us how it happened. Because it's a strange enough chance.

REITH: An advertisement in the *Morning Post* one day. British Broadcasting Company: Applications are invited for the following offices: General Manager, Secretary, Director of Programmes, Chief Engineer. Only those with first-class qualifications need apply. I wrote an application in the Cavendish Club, and then I did what I ought to have done before, looked up the name of the man this advertisement said would receive the applications. Having seen his name in *Who's Who*, I then went to the hall porter and persuaded him to allow me to recover this letter, and I added a P.S. – 'No doubt you would know some of my people in Aberdeen'. And that is how I got the job.

MUGGERIDGE: And why the BBC became what it did become. Because you shaped it, didn't you?

REITH: I suppose I did.

MUGGERIDGE: Well of course you did. I can't get it out of my mind, this picture of you, a young man coming to London from Scotland not so very long before, suddenly confronted with this enormous responsibility and accepting it. Did you never have doubts? Did you never think: Am I really qualified to exercise this incredible authority?

REITH: No. No, I don't – no, definitely not. I was going to say, no I don't think so, but I'll withdraw that and say definitely not.

MUGGERIDGE: And where did the certainty and the confidence come from?

REITH: Well, you could say it was derivative of self-confidence. An unjustified self-confidence maybe. I just felt I could – mark you, with the help of the Almighty, and I say that seriously. I say that the Almighty was there in my receiving that job and was there with me in my execution of the job. Have you got anything to say about that?

MUGGERIDGE: The only thing I'd say is this, that of course the ordinary person listening to that, not knowing you particularly well, would think: Surely a man who has as close a relation with the Almighty as that should have a certain humility, and that this is perhaps lacking.

REITH: You've got me on that.

MUGGERIDGE: You realized what an enormous thing the BBC was going to be, that it was going to change people's lives. How did you shape to the task of dealing with it?

REITH: With complete confidence. Is that the answer?

MUGGERIDGE: One part. Didn't it ever worry you to think that the logical outcome of the way you were looking at the future of broadcasting was to be, in effect, a monopoly?

REITH: No. I'd have been very worried otherwise. There were criticisms of the monopoly position before I started. They almost entirely disappeared within three or four years.

MUGGERIDGE: Well, honesty compels me to admit that I was one of the critics myself, and I was a critic because I thought that, however admirably conducted a monopoly might be, it would always in the end operate on the side of the established social order. Isn't that true?

REITH: I wouldn't admit that the BBC was operated by me on the side of the Establishment.

MUGGERIDGE: In essential points.

REITH: Do you mean political, or moral?

MUGGERIDGE: I mean in every way. I mean you in all good faith upheld a social system, a church, a government's policy – in all good faith, and there's no reason on earth why you shouldn't. But I see in that the danger of a monopoly.

REITH: Technically, I thought a monopoly was justifiable, but I was far, far more interested in the monopoly in terms of the

intellectual and ethical standard of the content of its programmes.

MUGGERIDGE: That would imply that the ethical standard and
the intellectual standard which you decided upon was to be the
prevailing standard.

REITH: Yes. Arrogant?

MUGGERIDGE: Self-confident.

REITH: Self-confident.

MUGGERIDGE: In the sense that you'd feel that you were
equipped to decide that. It has been said that when you picked
your staff, you satisfied yourself that they were Christians and
that their way of life was, in the conventional sense, respectable.

REITH: It's a nice story. It's partly true.

MUGGERIDGE: I bet you'd never have appointed me, for instance! If I'd applied.

REITH: Don't be too sure. People used to say that I put them
through the mangle. Have you ever been put through the
mangle?

MUGGERIDGE: In my day.

REITH: If a man was going to be concerned with the intellectual
or ethical side, as in talks and so forth, I was interested to know
what his views were on religion. I never said 'You must be a
Christian'. I asked their views. And got their views. If a man
were considerably like-minded to oneself obviously one would
still read his suggestions carefully, but one would know that
basically we were out for the same thing.

Political Pressures

MUGGERIDGE: I'd like to talk about one incident relating to
your position *vis-à-vis* the Government: and that was the
General Strike. Up to that point you'd had a relationship with
the Government which had never really been tested?

REITH: Not seriously.

MUGGERIDGE: Now it is tested seriously.

REITH: We had two or three days' warning and we were, to a
considerable extent, prepared for it. I lived quite near the Abbey
then, which meant that one was easily available to the Houses of
Parliament, and I got the newspaper leader in my house which

started the thing – the *Daily Mail* leader, do you remember?

MUGGERIDGE: Yes, I remember; which the printers refused to print.

REITH: I got the Prime Minister's view about the thing, and I suppose the Cabinet's view soon after that, and I myself broadcast those from my ordinary telephone in 6 Barton Street all over the country, because by that time all the transmitters were connected to headquarters. I had an interview with the Prime Minister the next morning. Stanley Baldwin was on the other side of the table, walking up and down, smoking a pipe, and I

was making a passionate appeal that the Government should
leave the BBC alone, and trust to me. And he said to me,
'Actually, I'm going to put this to the Cabinet in terms of
trusting the Managing Director. Is that all right?' I said, 'Yes,
fine.' Well, there were grumbles. The Cabinet weren't happy
about this; there was a division. The majority accepted it, the
minority, in particular Churchill and Birkenhead, didn't like it.
Hundreds of people already knew that the big power station
down the road was out of action, hundreds and thousands possibly, and the BBC broadcast the fact. Churchill fulminated
about that; broadcasting the success of the strikers. Do you see
the point?
MUGGERIDGE: Yes, I do. He, in other words, wanted the BBC
taken over by the Government to become an organ of propa-
ganda, is that right?
REITH: Absolutely.
MUGGERIDGE: And you resisted that?
REITH: I passed every single news bulletin. We were broadcasting news about the success of the strikers in particular, actions
where far more harm would have been caused if we hadn't, and
Churchill couldn't or wouldn't see that, and to the very end he
kept up his grumbling in the Cabinet, and with Stanley Baldwin. Now Ramsay MacDonald, who was Leader of the Opposition, asked me if I would allow the Archbishop of Canterbury
to speak. I had a letter delivered by hand from the Archbishop
enclosing what he wanted to say. It was just an appeal to the
Government to be – as the Archbishop thought, I suppose –
generous and large-minded, and not stand on the letter of the
law. So I sent it along to Baldwin, and was told, 'The Prime
Minister would rather you didn't do that.' Do you get the
terminology?
MUGGERIDGE: Oh yes.
REITH: We'd rather you didn't do it, and there was I, you see,
in the invidious position of having to arbitrate between the
Prime Minister of the country and the Archbishop of Canterbury, because I was so frightened of what Churchill would
make of it – get me?
MUGGERIDGE: Yes.
REITH: So I told the Archbishop I was sorry I wouldn't agree
to his broadcasting. Was I right? I think I was right, but I

hated it. I think the Prime Minister was mistaken.

MUGGERIDGE: I can see exactly why you did it, but at the same time you have to recognize that it's things like that which have led people to say that in the last resort the BBC has to accept the Government's direction.

Television

MUGGERIDGE: Did you see the potentialities of television from the beginning? Did you see what an enormous thing it was going to become?

REITH: I was frightened of it from the start.

MUGGERIDGE: Now why exactly?

REITH: There's an admission. Do you need to ask why?

MUGGERIDGE: I'd like to know.

REITH: You know yourself. And you could describe it better than I. May I ask you a question?

MUGGERIDGE: Yes, of course.

REITH: Has the introduction of television been to the benefit or the hurt of this country, of the world?

MUGGERIDGE: I would find that a terribly difficult thing to answer, particularly for me personally, because most of the great inventions of our time arouse in my mind at best a question mark. But now we come to the most extraordinary moment of all. You've created this great organization. You're in a position of very great authority, one of the three or four most powerful people of this country, and suddenly you walk out.

REITH: Look, I thought I had got a good organization, one that would stand up to anything, including war, including the development of television. In other words, I felt I was going to be to an extent unemployed, certainly not fully stretched, and I was frightened of that.

MUGGERIDGE: Your work was finished there?

REITH: My work was finished, provided always they chose the right man to succeed me.

MUGGERIDGE: Do you think that what you did was the right thing to do, or a mistake?

REITH: A frightful mistake.

MUGGERIDGE: You should have stayed?

REITH: Yes.

MUGGERIDGE: And you made the mistake for the sake of this

phrase that you use a tremendous lot in your writing and in talking, of being 'fully stretched'.

REITH: Yes, of every sort, physical and mental. Anyhow mental, particularly mental.

MUGGERIDGE: With no, as it were, slack at all?

REITH: Very, very little.

MUGGERIDGE: Is that really a sensible way to live?

REITH: No.

MUGGERIDGE: But it's your way.

REITH: I never learnt to live. You never believe me.

MUGGERIDGE: No, I don't. But that's an extraordinary thing to say – that you never learnt to live?

REITH: I mean it.

MUGGERIDGE: But it's –

REITH: Look – I did not realize until too late that life was for living. Now is that a bit clearer?

MUGGERIDGE: Did you actually just walk out of the BBC?

REITH: I stopped a presentation. I stopped anything by way of a farewell. My wife came for me, and we went down in the lift from the third floor, and across the hall to the entrance, or in this instance the exit, and there was standing the Senior Commissionaire who'd been on duty for the Company ever since it had started. My wife drew back there, went over and shook hands with him. A simple action. Too much for me. Beat me completely, and I went out of Broadcasting House, tears running down my cheeks. Then I did the most ridiculous macabre sort of journey round the countryside with two or three of the senior people whom I knew best. We had dinner at Droitwich, and after dinner, late dinner it was, very late, we went to the high-powered transmitters there, and I myself shut down the engines at midnight, and they asked me to sign my name in the book, the Visitors' Book, and I did. 'J. C. W. Reith, ex-BBC.'

Churchill

MUGGERIDGE: When the war came, Chamberlain offered you the Ministry of Information and without much enthusiasm you took it.

REITH: Yes.

MUGGERIDGE: You were to be our Goebbels.

REITH: Yes. That's what one was meant to be and ought to have been if one could only get the confidence of the Prime Minister.

MUGGERIDGE: Then in came Churchill.

REITH: In came Churchill.

MUGGERIDGE: And what happened then?

REITH: Walter Monckton and I were listening one night in the Ministry to a news bulletin and among the news items was that Mr Duff Cooper was appointed Minister of Information.

MUGGERIDGE: This was the first you heard, as Minister of Information. Incredible.

REITH: All right. Now, after two or three days I was sent for by Churchill. And he looked among his papers and he said, 'Oh, but I – I – I, well, there's something I want you to do.' He looked among the papers, you see, to find what it was he wanted me to do. 'I want you to go to the Ministry of Transport.' I said, 'All right, sir.'

MUGGERIDGE: Do you think that Churchill was hostile to you as a result of your previous disagreements when you were in the BBC?

REITH: Yes, he was. We were at a distance, there was no doubt about that. I saw him very, very occasionally. I was hardly aware of a Prime Minister through my term in the Ministry of Transport and the nearly two years, or whatever it was, in the Ministry of Works, hardly aware of a Prime Minister.

MUGGERIDGE: Did you like him? I mean, putting everything else aside.

REITH: No, I didn't. I disliked him – I think I disliked him very much – and distrusted him.

MUGGERIDGE: I see from your journal that you had an exchange of letters with Churchill after the war.

REITH: Yes.

MUGGERIDGE: And you explained to him various things. This is what you put in the last paragraph. 'I have, like you, a war mentality, and other qualities which should have commended themselves to you. Even in office I was nothing like fully stretched and I was completely out of touch with you. You could have used me in a way, and to an extent, you never realized. Instead of that there's been the sterility, humiliation and distress of all these years, eyeless in Gaza, without even the consolation Samson had in knowing it was his own fault, and that's how and where I still am.' That's your letter.

REITH: That's a good paragraph, isn't it?

MUGGERIDGE: Not bad. I see you got a telegram acknowledging it.

REITH: Oh, did I?

MUGGERIDGE: Now this is his letter to you, which is also extremely interesting. 'So far as my Administration's concerned, I've always admired your abilities and energy and it was with regret that I was not able to include you in the considerable reconstruction of the Government in February 1942. Several times since then I've considered you for various posts which became vacant, but I always encountered considerable opposition from one quarter or another on the grounds that you were difficult to work with ... If you think I can be of service to you at any time, pray let me know, for I'm very sorry that the fortunes of war should have proved so adverse to you, and I feel the State is in your debt.'

REITH: Good letter.

MUGGERIDGE: Yes.

REITH: But when he became Prime Minister again, he didn't do anything to discharge the debt of the State.

MUGGERIDGE: Isn't that always the case with politics?

REITH: Too often.

MUGGERIDGE: Putting aside the question of Churchill as a war leader, what do you think about him as a Prime Minister?

REITH: Do you want me to answer that?

MUGGERIDGE: Yes I do.

REITH: Ought I to?

MUGGERIDGE: I'm absolutely sure you ought to.

REITHH I doubt if England will recover from Churchill. Anyhow not for a long time. He gave no moral lead whatever after the war, when the country was as badly in need of it as it was during the war. I'm not talking now about Churchill as the wartime Prime Minister. I'm talking about him, in your terms, as an ordinary Prime Minister coming back. He gave no moral lead whatever. I would add this. Something has got to be done to put that right, and then the country may, I hope will, recover, and surely we ought to believe that it can and will.

MUGGERIDGE: Would I be right in saying that the principles of democracy applied in a particular institution or in a society are not particularly dear to you? Would I be right?

REITH: No. By and large, no, because this is what I would say, that I think on the whole I approve of, and endeavour to achieve, the principles of a democracy, but the processes – my golly – no.

MUGGERIDGE: In a word, what do you think is the best form of government?

REITH: Despotism tempered by assassination.

MUGGERIDGE: Is that what you had in the BBC when you were the boss?

REITH: Absolutely not. I had a most excellent and appreciated form of paternalism. Is that bad?

MUGGERIDGE: But no assassination?

REITH: No assassination – not that I was aware of.

MUGGERIDGE: There might have been a little here and there.

REITH: I believe profoundly in paternalism.

MUGGERIDGE: Yes, I know.

REITH: I am often – this is getting a bit personal – but I am often accused of having been autocratic and dictatorial, and all the rest of it, in the BBC. Was my management unkind, cruel? Or wicked in any way?

MUGGERIDGE: It's a terribly difficult question for me to answer because I wasn't there. But there are people who think it was.

REITH: Cruel?

MUGGERIDGE: They think that it was – intolerant.

REITH: Intolerance is not necessarily cruelty.

MUGGERIDGE: But it can easily become it, can't it?

REITH: Yes. Well, did it become it with me?

MUGGERIDGE: I don't think of you as a cruel man at all. But I think of you as a man who is prepared in the interests of efficiency to be autocratic.

REITH: Oh yes.

MUGGERIDGE: And I think that's a dangerous position. I think that's why when the devil tempted Christ, offered Him the Kingdoms of the earth, He very wisely turned them down. But you would have accepted them.

REITH: Maybe I would, maybe not.

Values

MUGGERIDGE: You regard your career as the story of a failure. Most people would regard it as a fantastic success story. Why do you consider it to be a failure?

REITH: Of course this is embarrassing, but let me just put one point to you. Can anyone really judge of success or failure other than the man or the woman concerned?

MUGGERIDGE: You mean that it has to be a subjective judgement?

REITH: All right, yes.

MUGERIDGE: You said earlier on, 'I haven't really lived. I've never learnt to live.' Now, I've puzzled and puzzled over this and I still don't really know what you mean by it.

REITH: Do you remember I said I'd never been young?

MUGGERIDGE: Yes.

REITH: That's the beginning of the explanation. And I suppose most of the rest of the explanation is that one has been far too serious-minded, far too desirous of getting the paper off the table quick. I've had few holidays in my life. Now that's sheer stupidity – lack of proportion.

MUGGERIDGE: In other words what you're saying is that you've been too intent on your main pursuits?

REITH: Yes.

MUGGERIDGE: And not sufficiently capable of putting them aside, relaxing, laughing, forgetting yourself.

REITH: Not nearly as much as I ought to have been. And that's why if I were sorry for anyone, it's for my wife, and to a lesser extent, but still a real extent, my son and daughter.

MUGGERIDGE: As we sit here tonight, in practically every home in this country this television thing will be switched on, and it will occupy for most of the people the evening hours. Anything to say about that at all?

REITH: It's a potential social menace of the first magnitude. Is that exaggeration?

MUGGERIDGE: Not in my eyes. Not in my eyes. Do you think there's been a moral – a lowering of moral standards in our society in recent years?

REITH: Yes, that's just what I was suggesting.

MUGGERIDGE: Do you think that the controllers of these mass communication media that have grown up in our time, all of them, could if they'd wished have checked this deterioration of moral standards?

REITH: You're talking about mass media generally?

MUGGERIDGE: Yes.

REITH: Yes, but they're not so minded, they haven't been so minded, or very few of them have.

MUGGERIDGE: And that's a condemnation of them or of our society or both?

REITH: Both.

MUGGERIDGE: This would seem to spell just decadence.

REITH: Is there no hope yet? Are we not permitted to hope? Has that been taken from us?

MUGGERIDGE: In other words the idea that our civilization has run into a decline would be to you an alien thought?

REITH: Yes. I believe that there is rescue coming.

MUGGERIDGE: But from where?

REITH: I don't know. But I still believe it.

MUGGERIDGE: After all, civilizations in the past have declined, have disappeared. Why shouldn't ours?

REITH: You have the Roman Empire in mind, haven't you?

MUGGERIDGE: Yes. Let me read from your rectorial address:

'On that hard pagan world, disgust and secret loathing fell.
Deep weariness and sated lust made human life a hell.'

It's my conviction that that could happen to us in these islands.

REITH: And here is my comment and the burden, I suppose, of what I'm trying to say to you. For God's sake prevent it happening here.

Happiness

The sister-in-law of a friend of Dr Johnson was imprudent enough once to claim in his presence that she was happy. He pounced on her hard, remarking in a loud, emphatic voice that, if she was indeed the contented being she professed herself to be, then her life gave the lie to every research of humanity; for she was happy without health, without beauty, without money and without understanding. It was rough treatment, for which Johnson has been much criticized, though it should be remembered that he spoke as an eighteenth-century man, before our present preoccupation with happiness as an enduring condition of human life became prevalent. Actually I think I see his point.

There is something quite ridiculous and even indecent in an individual *claiming* to be happy. Still more a people or a nation making such a claim. The pursuit of happiness, included along with life and liberty in the American Declaration of Independence as an inalienable right, is without any question the most fatuous which could possibly be undertaken. This lamentable phrase 'the pursuit of happiness' (arrived at, incidentally, almost by accident on the spur of the moment because the Founding Fathers jibbed at the defence of property as an inalienable right) is responsible for a good part of the ills and miseries of the modern world.

To pursue happiness, individually or collectively, as a conscious aim is the surest way to miss it altogether; as is only too tragically evident in countries like Sweden and America where happiness has been most ardently pursued and where the material circumstances usually considered conducive to happiness have been most effectively constructed. The Gardarene swine were doubtless in pursuit of happiness when they hurled themselves to destruction over the cliff. Today the greater part of mankind, led by the technologically most advanced, are similarly bent, and if they persist will assuredly meet a similar fate. The pursuit of happiness, in any case, soon resolved itself into the pursuit of pleasure – something quite different.

Pleasure is but a mirage of happiness – a false vision of shade and refreshment seen across parched sand.

Where, then, does happiness lie? In forgetfulness, not indulgence, of the self. In escape from sensual appetites, not in their satisfaction. We live in a dark, self-enclosed prison which is all we see or know if our glance is fixed ever downwards. To lift it upwards, becoming aware of the wide, luminous universe outside – this alone is happiness.

At its highest level such happiness is the ecstasy which mystics have inadequately described. At more humdrum levels it is human love; the delights and beauties of our dear earth, its colours and shapes and sounds; the enchantment of understanding and laughing, and all other exercise of such faculties as we possess; the marvel of the meaning of everything, fitfully glimpsed, inadequately expounded, but ever-present.

Such is happiness: not compressible into a pill; not translatable into a sensation; lost to whoever would grasp it to himself alone; not to be gorged out of a trough, or torn out of another's body, or paid into a bank, or driven along on an auto-route, or fired in gun-salutes, or discovered in the stratosphere. Existing, intangible, in every true response to life, and absent in every false one; propounded through the centuries in every noteworthy word and thought and deed; expressed in art and literature and music; in vast cathedrals and tiny melodies; in everything that is harmonious, and in the unending heroism of imperfect men reaching after perfection.

When Pastor Bonhoeffer was taken off by his Nazi guards to be executed, as I have read, his face was shining with happiness, to the point that even those poor clowns noted it. In that place of darkest evil he was the happiest man – he the executed. 'For you it is an end,' he told his executioners, 'but for me a beginning.' I find this an image of supreme happiness.

The Goat

Are you seriously suggesting on this programme that David Lloyd George was a monogamist?

Failure

For myself I consider in all sincerity that I have been an abysmal failure. Over the last forty years I must have written, at a modest estimate, on an average some 5,000 words a week, or, say, a quarter of a million words a year. The number I have spoken on radio or television I dare not contemplate. In all, ten million written words, of which so very, very few, if any, may be considered as having more than a momentary validity. Even the qualities I consider admirable – such as self-abnegation, loving kindness, unworldliness, spirituality – I have but poorly, if at all, exemplified. I never heard of anyone of any account who believed he had been successful. Tolstoy, for instance, was so conscious of failure that, as he recounts in his autobiography, he found it necessary to hide away a rope that lay about in his study for fear of hanging himself with it. Shakespeare again (perhaps foreseeing the invention of television) wrote of himself with deep dissatisfaction :

> Tis true, alas, I have been here and there,
> and made myself a motley to the view. . . .

The reason is obvious. It is only possible to succeed at second-rate pursuits – like becoming a millionaire or a prime minister, winning a war, seducing beautiful women, flying through the stratosphere, or landing on the moon. First-rate pursuits – involving, as they must, trying to understand what life is about and trying to convey that understanding – inevitably result in a sense of failure. A Napoleon, a Churchill, a Roosevelt can feel themselves to be successful, but never a Socrates, a Pascal, a Blake. Understanding is for ever unattainable. Therein lies the inevitability of failure in embarking upon its quest, which is none the less the only one worthy of serious attention.

Of course I am well aware that there can be a sort of vanity and egotism in a sense of failure – for instance those Dostoevsky heroes who glory in their own abasement. It is dangerous to reason that, since all great men are conscious of being failures, therefore if I am conscious of being a failure I am a great man. One must watch out. All the same the Christian notion that the weak are strong and the foolish wise and the meek see God is sound enough. By the same token the successful are failures, and those who grasp in true humility the fallacy of success are, like the poor, blessed.

Animals

I feel an instinctive loathing of this idea that animals must be treated with complete contempt in order that they may serve men. Don't misunderstand me. The position that I'm stating, as I am well aware, is incapable of a logical application. I'm only putting in a proviso that I notice in the society in which I live, as I get older, a sort of attitude towards animals, that they are purely for our food, purely to serve our interests, and that we can treat them as we like. And I think that this will be very dangerous because ultimately it will rebound against human beings. Blake said, 'A robin redbreast in a cage puts high heaven in a rage.' Marvellous. Marvellous couplet. Profoundly true. A robin redbreast in a cage puts high heaven in a rage. I agree.

Tynan

We called our parrot Tynan, but it didn't do any good.

Twilight of Empire

India revisited

When I was twenty, the world seemed a place to explore. Subsequently, God knows my ageing carcass has been hauled about this earth's surface often enough. Even so, that first occasion, waving goodbye to everyone and everything I knew, and making off, remains unforgettable. On a cold, misty December day in the year 1924 I sailed for India.

After forty years I returned there. In the intervening time the world had changed out of all recognition – and I with it. Yet at first glance there seemed no difference in the people and the scene which so long ago had so enchantingly contrasted with the south London suburb where I lived with my family; and Cambridge where I'd spent four unprofitable years. It was an embodiment of all I'd ever imagined about the tropics and the Orient. The same backwaters, the same boats and boatmen. Of course, I was young when I first came and, I suppose, innocent. Everything was new and fresh. Was it really as smiling a place as it had seemed in my memory? Travel, I know, narrows the mind, and the passing years dull the judgement. Even so I was still enchanted.

As an undergraduate I'd agreed, as a result of a casual encounter with a missionary, to teach at a Christian college at Alwaye in what was then Travancore and is now Kerala in the southern tip of India. The terms of employment were indeterminate. I had only the vaguest notion of where Alwaye was, and I was by no means particularly a Christian. In those far-off days we tried to convey our contempt for the world and its ways by despising success, and cultivating improvidence – a bizarre sort of romanticism I suppose. But I had no thought of embarking on a career: it was going somewhere, anywhere; and doing something, anything.

But, of course, one forgets. On that first journey there must have been many places along the way: a great variety of impressions. The one that sticks in my mind is arriving at Alleppey. So many brown faces and bodies crowding round and, as it seemed, shouting at me. And I, a white man, a sahib, in a suit and a topee. I remember the feeling I had of panic and even terror – the sense of isolation. At the college it was, of course, different. But I couldn't but wonder how I was going to be received this time, returning after so long an interval – a stranger.

MUGGERIDGE: It's marvellous to be back. . . . The river – you go straight down there to the river, don't you?
INDIAN: That's right. Straight down.
MUGGERIDGE: I think I shall go and bathe. The river seems to have maintained itself through the years?
INDIAN: The one thing they didn't change.
MUGGERIDGE: Yes – no change in the river.

There's plenty of change in me though. I used to swim across and back so easily, but not now. Half-way was quite enough, and even that partly perhaps to show off. It's extraordinary how large a part this river played in my life at Alwaye. Besides bathing in it I had a little boat of my own to paddle along. Whenever I've thought of Alwaye, it's the river I've seen in my mind's eye. Well, now I've seen it again with my other eye.

What a joy to find old colleagues and students; so many of them. Familiar faces though, like mine, grown old.

INDIAN: I remember one very interesting incident when you were teaching here – I was a student then. You had a contempt for annotation –
MUGGERIDGE: Yes, correct!
INDIAN: And one Indian professor, a Brahmin gentleman, visited the college – he was author of so many annotations. He visited the college, and he gave a lecture on Shakespeare; and you presided over that meeting. And in your presidential remarks you said something like this: 'If I go to heaven, which I very much doubt, I shall ask of God one favour. And that is to send Shakespeare down to earth again, and make him sit a Madras University examination in Shakespeare, just for the fun of seeing him fail.'
MUGGERIDGE: Well, I'm sure Shakespeare would fail.

INDIAN: Yes, I'm sure too.

MUGGERIDGE: The question is: whether God would pass an examination in theology? What do you think about that? It's an awkward question.

I've never been such a regular letter-writer as I was at Alwaye: long ones home every week, meticulously describing my life, thoughts and emotions. With preposterous conceit I asked my father to keep them for posterity. He did keep them, but only for me, not for posterity. In one, soon after my arrival, I described a typical Alwaye day. 'I get up at five-thirty – no staying-in-bed problem. As soon as one wakes one's only desire is to bathe, normally in the river. Then at six-thirty my servant, Kuruvilla, brings me tea and bananas. I read for a while – lately Whitman and Tagore. From seven to nine I prepare lectures; and between nine-thirty and one I teach. In the afternoon I sleep till three; read from three to five, and then take exercise – either tennis or a walk, followed by another swim in the river. It's a sort of monastic existence, but I quite like it. My servant's a good soul, but a perfect fool. Once I was smoking on my bed and a box of matches went off and burnt my hand. I shouted to Kuruvilla for ointment. He brought me first Brasso and then toothpaste. On another occasion he used communion wine to light the primus.'

Education, the great mumbo-jumbo of the age, was as avidly in demand in India as elsewhere. It's conducted in a foreign language – English, and related to an alien culture. Little Indian boys used to be taught the names and dates of the kings and queens of England; sometimes even the promontories round our coast. Our Alwaye classrooms had no sides to them. Holding forth one could see the green paddy-fields and the brown shining bodies of the men and women working in them. Their weird, echoing songs broke into counterfeit words like the sound of the sea in a dark cave. Senior students, such as mine, ploughed through the Elizabethan dramatists and the Lake poets. 'Dryden,' I would proclaim, having culled the phrase from some outline or short history of English literature, 'found English brick and left it marble.'

Education was about the worst thing we did to India; and,

appropriately enough, contributed to our departure. Wasn't it predominantly enraged and unemployed graduates who chased us out, hurtling after us curses and copies of the *Oxford Book of English Verse*?

Teaching always bored me as much as being taught, and I escaped with relief whenever possible from the classroom. On 19 April 1925 I wrote to my parents: 'One of the pleasantest things about living here is to go by boat through the backwaters, not a motor boat – but one of the primitive ancient ones, propelled along by boatmen. You stretch out under a wicker shelter; fall asleep to the boat's rhythm; then wake up to find everything bathed in moonlight, with boatmen singing a kind of chant as, leaning on their poles, they walk up and down the whole length of the boat.'

I belonged to the generation that was still wild about nature. We looked at sunsets and sunrises with appropriate rapture; we tramped about the countryside; we sought our remote eminences; we paced along moonlit beaches. We even read Wordsworth. To one so conditioned this Travancore countryside was a sort of ecstasy. At all times and in all seasons glowing with luxuriance. I thought when I first saw it – and I think still – that it's one of the most beautiful places in the whole wide world.

Living as I did almost exclusively among Indians, wearing Indian dress, eating Indian food, I had little contact with the Raj and its sahibs. Travancore was an Indian state, ruled over by a maharajah. This was Indian India. The all-powerful Government seemed very far away. Its representative was the British Resident, Cotton, who, tired perhaps of the local sahibs, occasionally invited me, a non-sahib, to visit him. 'Cotton,' I wrote home, 'is the focus here of all snobbishness as far as the local English community are concerned. An invitation from him is equivalent to one from the Palace. When he drives to the capital, Trivandrum, the river ferries are held up in case he should be delayed even for a few minutes. Indians fall over themselves to get into his good graces. His house, Bolghatty, is like a south-sea island, with palm trees, and a breeze always blowing. I quite expected to see darkies and hear banjoes playing. Instead there was an Indian brass band, somewhat mournfully and tunelessly grinding out "Sussex by the Sea". Cotton was waiting for me at the jetty: a solid man, well turned out, wearing stays I should suppose; everything in perfect order. Ice in the drinks – a great rarity in these parts; two not so young ladies, elegantly dressed; and some sort of visiting newspaper-owner with a small goatee beard, who dilated upon how everywhere he'd found the "natives" loyal. There's something false, decayed, hopeless, about the whole English way of life in India.'

After two years at Alwaye I had become ill; and leaving India was a relief – something I'd looked forward to and even longed for. The heat and dust and hopelessness had become oppressive. Yet mixed with a sense of relief was a kind of regret which remained with me. One may discount the old bromide about India's spirituality, and still realize that in some mysterious way eternity looms larger on these shores than elsewhere. In Alwaye I thought I caught a glimpse of eternity which, I am thankful to say, through subsequent vicissitudes and follies has never been totally eclipsed.

It was ten years before I again saw India, and then it was a different me and a different India – Calcutta, surely one of the ugliest and most squalid cities in the world. Created by the English on a swamp, its warm, humid air suggests a swamp still. I had become a journalist – a dubious trade. My part was to sit at a typewriter, tapping out portentous editorial pronouncements. 'It is to be hoped that these two great peoples, the English and the Indians, whose destinies etc. etc., history has etc. etc., will find it possible etc. etc., to the enrichment of both their etc. etc.' – what rot!

Newsprint like ourselves is mortal, and in a matter of decades moulders away. Perhaps fortunately. Dust to dust. Oh printed word, where is thy sting? It takes a wise editorialist to recognize his own editorials. Browsing about among the editorial columns of these papers, I ask myself which of them I wrote. Did I for instance write, 'If the disarmament discussions have produced as their only obvious consequence the determination in some countries to seek peace through the argument of increased equipment for war, this itself by its bitter incongruity is forcing statesmen here and there to seek means of renewing the discussions for some wider aim.' Honesty compels me to admit that I might have.

The main preoccupation of Indian newspapers during this period was of course the question of independence or swaraj. Now I see that on 22 November 1934 there was an enormous news story with a heading right across the main news page, a most unusual thing, referring to the report of the Joint Select Parliamentary Committee in Westminster on Indian constitutional reform. And the editorialist, perhaps me, describes this 'as a state paper of the highest historical importance, whose language is adequate to the gravity of the scene'. Neatly put. But who today remembers or cares anything about this state paper of the highest historical importance? Grave the scene may have been, but it was clearly irrelevant to anything that had, could or would happen, in India or elsewhere.

Today, of course, the Calcutta *Statesman* is a rather different paper: 'home' is no longer England but India. It still has plenty of Joint Parliamentary Committees, but they're domestically produced. And there are no knighthoods any more in Bengal.

'Let this monument erected by the voluntary donations of thousands and thousands of his subjects throughout his Indian Empire, the rich giving of their wealth, and the poor of their poverty, bear witness to their grateful memory of his virtues and his might. He was the father of his people. His sceptre ruled one fifth of the dwellers on earth, his reign was a blessing to his well-beloved India, an example to the great and an encouragement to the humble. And his name shall be handed down from father to son throughout all ages, as a mighty emperor, a merciful ruler, and a great Englishman.'

That inscription was written, presumably without a smile, in 1911, the year of the Great Durbar, and related to King Edward VII. It indicates the mood of confidence which animated the British rulers of India so shortly before, as it turned out, their final departure. It was in such a mood that they set about constructing what they thought was going to be their own enduring capital, New Delhi, whose walls were rising in my time.

On seeing the plans of New Delhi, Clemenceau is said to have remarked that it would make an even finer ruin than the six or seven other ruined capitals in the vicinity. So far, the walls still stand, though the British have gone taking their Viceroy with them. There are no ruling princes to sit in the chamber designed for them. A bewigged Mr Speaker presides over the Lok Sabha, where honourable and right honourable members debate in accordance with the Westminster rules. In addition to the *Oxford Book of English Verse,* we gave India the Ballot Box. Likewise an inappropriate gift and already second- if not third-hand when presented.

Journalists have to follow governments as sharks swim in the wake of big liners. I followed the Government to Simla, one of the sharks to whom occasionally officials would throw a morsel of news. It was my business to convey, explain and expound to the Viceroy's distant subjects the policies and purposes of his government, if any. Who, I wondered, would be occupying Viceregal Lodge now that there was no Viceroy? Who the Commander-in-Chief's house, and all those official residences carefully graded by the Office of Works so that one could tell at a glance the status or salary of the occupant? Simla without a Viceroy – inconceivable! What astonishing if not crazy arrogance for the alien government of a sub-continent to transfer itself to this mountain eyrie just because some of its top personnel found the heat oppressive in the plains below. As though England should be ruled in the summer months from the Dolomites, with Whitehall and all the requisite clerks and files transferred there accordingly.

Simla at least we English created. It is our Taj Mahal. Royal Tunbridge Wells in the shadow of the Himalayas – Cheltenham on the world's roof – as English as marmalade. There is even a bandstand where on Saturday evenings a military band used to play selections from Gilbert and Sullivan and Colonel Bogey, The British Grenadiers, echoing away towards Tibet. Nothing anywhere to suggest it was India, except, of course, Indians.

With the Raj over and the Government gone, I think I half expected to find Simla deserted. Not so. Offices and residences all occupied, typewriters tapping away as merrily as ever, files circulating, peons dozing, brown burrasahibs borne to and fro in rickshaws as white ones once had been. The white sahib has been dethroned, but his spirit goes marching on. In the Gaiety Theatre amateur theatricals still being rehearsed, but in Indian

English.

'Then, old chap, it is this, I love your wife.'

'Oh, that.'

'What do you say, old boy?'

'You're a bounder, sir. I've a good mind to give you a sound thrashing.'

'What a lot of twit. Are you going, old chap?'

'I bloody am – damn everything.'

How strange it would have seemed to Gandhi – he who recommended salvation through the spinning wheel and homespun, all the ancient Indian ways!

It was a strange sensation to saunter up the winding empty drive to the Viceregal Lodge – no sentries now, no attentive ADCs. Those gilt-edged invitation cards, once so thankfully received, so triumphantly waved in the faces of the bearded Sikh bodyguard. 'His Excellency requests the pleasure. . . .' His Excellency did not request in vain.

And now, shutting one's eyes outside the main entrance, one can imagine everything as it was before. Those garden parties: the guest list extending down to clergymen and even missionaries, to the humbler grades of Indian officials with their wives in coloured saris. The Viceroy – Lord Willingdon in my time – in grey frock-coat and matching top hat, a slight stooping figure, the Vicereine ebullient in mauve, with a sunshade, smiling to left and right that toothy unrecognizing smile of great personages. The gardens and the lawns remain, but the people have gone. No more garden parties ever, I should suppose, in this place. Inside, it's like a stage being dismantled when a play's run is over. The lights are out, players and audience have dispersed. These sometime corridors of power are empty and deserted, they are rolling up the carpets in Viceregal Lodge, and we shan't see them spread out again in our time.

How extraordinary to have been the Viceroy, living in this country house among these mountains, with, below, the teeming plains of India where a fifth of the human race live and die, he their absolute ruler, responsible not to them, but to a parliament thousands of miles away, under grey skies and by a grey river in England. I saw an empire ruled from here, and have lived to see that empire and all its trappings disappear as though they'd never been. Now they're largely forgotten, and only linger on in minds like mine with their own bizarre reasons for remembering.

Here we, the guests invited to dinner, lined up, the ladies smoothing down their dresses in preparation for the curtsies into which they were shortly going to plunge, the gentlemen making sure that all their orders and decorations were correctly placed, that their fly buttons were fastened and that their braces weren't showing. Then the band begins to play, and there's a shout. Their Excellencies! And in they come, the frail Viceroy bent more than ever with the weight of hardware that's fastened about his person. The Vicereine still in mauve, this time an evening dress with a red sash across it and a coronet on her head. They pass along the line of guests, a friendly word for everyone, an ADC at their elbow to make sure that they don't forget a name. And there, far away at the end of the line, is Muggeridge Sahib in a tail coat, no decorations, no orders, but very conscious of the three chota pegs he had before leaving to keep up his spirits; holding his own, just. Then when all this rigmarole at last is over, in we joyously go to dinner.

How extraordinary it is to find the most important prop of all still miraculously in its place in the middle of all this debris – the Viceroy's throne, with the silver footstool in front of it. I must say I never thought I should ever sit in it. The Vicereine on her throne on one side of him and the Governor of the Punjab on the other. And before him milling about, rajahs and maharajas, hopeful of some extra gun salutes, officers hopeful of promotion, officials dreaming of honours to come – CBEs, Stars of India, perhaps the Bath itself. The Viceroy was in a position to satisfy them all. Seated on his throne he was the repository of power and the fount of patronage. Let's see how he struck me at the time. In my diary there's an entry: 6 May 1935 'At Viceregal Lodge yesterday, spoke first with the Vicereine, Lady Willingdon, a noisy, energetic, atrocious woman, yet not without a certain vulgar fascination. At this point an ADC hove in sight, to take me away and over to the Viceroy. Somewhat unusual to be moved straight from her square to his. I was duly flattered. Willingdon tremendously like an old beau in a Restoration comedy. With unusual animation he began by saying (and one almost expected him to take a pinch of snuff and flick his handkerchief), "You know people say this country's difficult to govern, actually it's not, you know. I find it perfectly easy to get on with these fellows. I've found it the easiest country in the world to govern." In all the circumstances a pretty extraordinary statement, but I let it pass. "I believe in Providence," he went on. "But for that I'd never have been able to carry on." A grey old fellow, full of egotism, but with a kind of charm, not in the least pompous, absolute ruler over some hundreds of millions of Indians, and a believer in Providence.' Alas, poor Viceroy, yet why 'alas'? The end of power is always more exhilarating than its beginning. I much prefer Napoleon on St Helena to Napoleon being crowned by the Pope in Notre Dame, Hitler in his tank-tangled bunker to the *sieg-heils* of Nuremberg. In the days of its functioning, I used to hate this popinjay court up here. Its disappearance into furniture vans is one court the less. Let the bell which summoned the Viceroy's guests to dinner toll for it now.

No one, apart from a few power maniacs and fools, allows public affairs to take precedence over private ones. Thus I'm delighted to note in my Simla diaries that my own personal affairs loomed much larger than the news I was supposed to be covering. King George V's Jubilee, which must have been a tremendous affair, seems to have passed me by. For one bare mention of the King George V Jubilee there are pages and pages about becoming acquainted with Amrita Shergil, now generally recognized as the outstanding modern Indian painter – then of course largely unknown. She's dead and I'm old, and our brief but intense intimacy mattered to no one. A portrait of me by Amrita now hangs in the National Gallery of Modern Art in Delhi, in a room dedicated to her work. She was gay, alive, beautiful – a combination of qualities not unduly plentiful in Simla, or for that matter anywhere. She studied at the Ecole des Beaux Arts in Paris and sometimes, rather affectedly I'm afraid, we'd speak French together. I remember how when she came to see me off, at the station at Simla when I went away, she said there'd be some '*beaux moments*'. I agreed, and I never saw her again.

Cemeteries are likely to be the most enduring of all the British Raj's memorials. I find the graves that we left behind us more poignant and more eloquent than other traces of our short occupancy of India. Cemeteries lashed by monsoon rains, baked by ferocious suns, under so alien skies. Or up here in Simla, on a quiet hillside. Many of the sahibs died young. Mortality was high among them in the early days. Whatever brought them to India in the first place – cupidity, restlessness, ambition, missionary zeal, or just chance – they served the country and its people according to their lights. I never liked them, they were not my sort of person – for the most part self-satisfied and self-important, and at all levels, from the private soldiers to the Viceroy, corrupted, as it seemed to me, by the excessive subservience of their Indian underlings. Yet those whose mortal remains here in Simla, and elsewhere, will abide in India for ever need not be abashed among the ghosts of other conquerors. They were few, some ten thousand. And they kept four hundred million Indians in approximate order and security and, by the abysmal standards of this land, fed. On the last page of my Simla diary I wrote the words 'Twilight of Empire'. I never saw the morning or the noontide. Only the twilight. Nor did I stay to see night fall, but made off elsewhere.

Nationalism

The division of the world into sovereign nationalist states is an outmoded thing. We may not live to see the end of it but it's going.

Equality

On the one hand we are telling people that it is absolutely wrong that there should be any inequality, and any honest man must assent to that. On the other hand, we are asking people to save, to provide for their future, to pursue their own interests and ends. Now these two things are, in fact, incompatible.

The Death of Nehru

I was in Travancore when Nehru died. It was quite extraordinary. We were driving along and didn't know, and we suddenly saw these processions that were forming spontaneously; they just formed into processions going nowhere. Everyone was completely silent and you heard this pat-pat-pat of feet, bare feet on the dusty roads, and that is all you heard. Nehru was in a way the last Viceroy. We unified the country and he was the last Viceroy. Now he was dead and that was the end of it.

Looking back with Leonard Woolf

Remembering Virginia

Virginia Woolf wrote with great intensity and effort, reaching a kind of ecstasy of inspiration, and then correspondingly falling into the pit of despair. As we know from her journal, the strain of her writing taxed her precarious mental equilibrium, while stopping writing was liable to bring on bouts of depression. It was an appalling dilemma whose fluctuations in all their poignancy can be read as she recorded them day by day in her journal.

WOOLF (reading diary): This is an interesting piece because it's what she wrote about finishing *The Waves*. 'Here in the few minutes that remain I must record, heaven be praised, the end of *The Waves*. I wrote the words "oh death" fifteen minutes ago, having reeled across the last ten pages with some moments of such intensity and intoxication that I seemed only to stumble after my own voice; after some sort of speaker as when I was mad.'

MUGGERIDGE: Virginia's intermittent bouts of madness were the converse side of her genius – the sombre background against which her sparkle, her subtlety, her originality, her gaiety, her delight in people and companionship shone the more brightly. For you, Leonard, the alternations must have been an appalling strain: sitting over meals for hours coaxing her to eat, dreading a step in the night, hiding away the means of self-destruction.

WOOLF: She had alternations of what are called manic depression now. She could be very excited and exhilarated in a completely irrational way, talking in this state for days, until she became completely incoherent. I mean, the words meant nothing. Then she would fall into a coma, lasting for two days; and finally come to, and gradually recover.

MUGGERIDGE: It must have been absolutely hellish for you. But I have always been tremendously interested in the connection between her mental collapse and her writing. There must have

been, of course, a connection.

WOOLF: I think it really is that her sort of genius was connected with her sort of madness and that you could see it in the way that her mind worked when she was perfectly sane. First of all in her own conversation she would suddenly do what I called 'leave the ground'. Suddenly she would begin telling one something quite ordinary, an incident that she'd seen in the street or something like that; and when her mind seemed to get completely off the ground she would give the most fascinating and amusing description of something fantastic, quite unlike anything that anyone other than herself would have thought of, which would last for about five or ten minutes.

MUGGERIDGE: Of course that is what is meant by inspiration. We have all felt it to a minute degree that one is racing after some meaning that is ahead of us.

WOOLF: Yes. And not only that. I think that very rarely, when one is writing, suddenly a thought or phrase comes into one's mind which seems to be out of one's control; that one hadn't thought of it oneself. And I think that, with people who are inclined to be mad and also inclined to be geniuses, that goes on with much greater intensity.

MUGGERIDGE: Blake was an example.

WOOLF: Yes.

MUGGERIDGE: I mean he barely understood himself. But then, Leonard, how did it happen that this ecstasy was combined with this black despair, and led her in the end to take her own life?

WOOLF: I think it was an exaggeration of what everyone feels. You get out of bed one day on the wrong side and you're miserable, and the next day you get out of bed in the morning, and you're exhilarated. And if you're exhilarated, it's ten to one that you will be depressed before the evening. My nurse always used to say that there'll be tears before the evening if I was very excited. You see, I think that exhilaration of her inspiration, of her writing, was followed by a depression. Both were not really under her control and much more violent than ordinary people's. Her depression would become so great that she would think life was no longer worth living.

MUGGERIDGE: And end it.

WOOLF: And end it.

MUGGERIDGE: What do you feel about suicide?

WOOLF: I think it's a lamentable thing as it happens, but I think if life isn't worth living one ought to commit suicide. I can't feel that I would, but I've got no objection to other people doing it if they want to.

MUGGERIDGE: You don't feel that society should set its face against it?

WOOLF: No.

MUGGERIDGE: Which of course has been the Christian attitude, hasn't it? You don't approve of that?

WOOLF: No, I think it's absurd. Don't you?

MUGGERIDGE: Well, I don't actually, no, because I think that you've got to — that society must discourage people from doing this.

WOOLF: Yes, but it's absurd. If you commit suicide, you're

done for, you can't be punished. You're only punished for not succeeding in committing suicide.

MUGGERIDGE: I agree that it's illogical, but it still remains clear to me that it is absolutely terrible that such a thing should happen.

WOOLF: Oh, it's appalling – and also the process. If one had seen it, as I did, seen it with one's own eyes. It's only if there's been an appalling amount of mental torture such as she went through when she felt that she was going mad and that she couldn't control her thoughts, it was only when she got to that stage that she committed suicide, and of course the process of getting to that stage was absolutely appalling to – to watch.

MUGGERIDGE: Agony, I should think. But you must have been aware all the time that this was liable to happen.

WOOLF: Oh yes. As soon as I realized what it was, of course, it was what one had to guard against. Not that at any moment she would have committed suicide, because that wasn't the case. The process by which anyone with that mental disease, because it really is a disease, reaches the suicide stage is quite a long process. At times she would be perfectly all right and walk out into the garden without any danger of committing suicide. It was only after one of these long attacks in which she got more and more depressed and couldn't sleep or write, or work or see people, then she felt that she would never recover and would try to commit suicide.

MUGGERIDGE: Was it the price she paid for producing her books?

WOOLF: I think it was really.

Judges

Most judges talk drivel the entire time.

Education

I dislike education. I think it's an over-rated thing. On the whole educated people are the most stupid.

Pilgrim's Progress

A discussion with Aneurin Bevan

MUGGERIDGE: I read *Pilgrim's Progress* again the other day, and I was enormously struck by how it stands up. What a perfect image it is of human life.

BEVAN: Well, Mr Muggeridge, I'm afraid I don't agree with that. You see, it's all so simple. You always know that Faithful is going to be faithful. You always know that Mr Greatheart is never going to give in; and life's much more complex than that.

MUGGERIDGE: Well, don't forget the case of Christian himself, Mr Bevan. After all he changes all right and his character develops. He is led astray and then he finds the way again, and he listens to false counsel and then comes to realize it's false.

BEVAN: Yes, he does; but then you see we read the names. One is called Fearful, the other is called Ignorance. There's no suspense in the book, there's no tension. It's not epic drama, it's melodrama, precisely because of that fact.

MUGGERIDGE: I wouldn't agree with that at all because one does have the feeling of anxiety. Is he going to make it? Is he going to get to the end? Just as one does if one reads a play like *Macbeth* for the thirtieth time. One knows perfectly well that Duncan is going to be murdered, and at the same time anxiety is there.

BEVAN: Ah, but in the case of *Macbeth* you have a drama. In the case of *Macbeth* you have conflicting forces inside people as well as outside people. The great soliloquy of Lady Macbeth is itself evidence of remorse, of tension, of apprehension of the future, but it's inside her. What Bunyan has done is personify the qualities of men in different personalities.

MUGGERIDGE: I quite agree that he intended an allegory; but the miracle of *Pilgrim's Progress* is that it turned into the first novel in the English language.

BEVAN: It may be the first novel, but it is not, in terms of the

modern scene, sufficiently illuminating or rewarding.

MUGGERIDGE: I think that's the great point of difference between you and me. You think that the modern scene has invalidated *Pilgrim's Progress* and I think that it remains *as* valid in the modern scene and indeed in any conceivable human scene.

BEVAN: It never was any good because in the first place it was too obvious, in the second place it simplifies life to the point where it is of no assistance to anyone, and in the third place it becomes exceedingly dull.

MUGGERIDGE: I don't agree with that at all. To me it's fascinating, and it's fascinating because I get a living sense of human beings.

BEVAN: I'm bound to say that if Mr Muggeridge can find *Pilgrim's Progress* fascinating he's a very easy man to write for.

MUGGERIDGE: I'm not alone. This book has been found fascinating by millions of people, literally millions of people.

BEVAN: I wonder. It's a sort of thing that you have as part of your furniture. I expect you can visit many homes and you see *Pilgrim's Progress* there with uncut leaves.

MUGGERIDGE: Well, my children loved reading it, I can assure you of that, and furthermore it's been translated into every language. Now I can't believe that all that would have been undertaken merely, as Mr Bevan suggests, in order to have a respectable book to put on a shelf. That's beyond my powers of imagination.

BEVAN: Now may I make another point about *Pilgrim's Progress* which in fact I think is very rarely made. I think Bunyan himself was not writing primarily a religious tract. He was writing a political tract. He says at the beginning. 'A man clothed with rags, standing in a certain place, a book in his hand, and a great burden upon his back.' Well, of course, that burden is said to be sin, but over and over again it is obviously the burden of poverty of which he is speaking. He is a poor man fighting against established institutions.

MUGGERIDGE: I was waiting for this to happen. You see we're moving on. Bunyan has got to be a Bevanite. That's the truth of it.

BEVAN: Wouldn't he – wouldn't he be now if he were alive?

MUGGERIDGE: I once looked up his biography and the curious thing about him is that it's not even by any means certain that he was on the Parliamentary side in the Civil War. I doubt whether Mr Bevan would have been.

BEVAN: ... malevolence, Mr Muggeridge.

MUGGERIDGE: I love this book because it transcends the things you've mentioned. I quite agree that Bunyan was poor; I quite

agree that he went to prison; I quite agree that he was anguished that people should be in poverty; but I don't believe
that the burden that he carried on his back was his burden of
poverty, and I don't believe that his beautiful raiment, when he
lost his rags, was provided by the Ministry of Health.

BEVAN: Why do you think he was put in prison?

MUGGERIDGE: He was put in prison because he was naturally, as
all good men are, a nonconformist.

BEVAN: No, no, no. He was put in prison because people of his
way of thinking were regarded as rebels. He uses the language of
levellers. It's a protest; and if you notice, when he comes to
certain cities he is taken secretly to one of the friends who is
known to the others. There is a conspiratorial quality about the
book which is only credible when you consider it as a political
pamphlet, shared by a number of people who are conspiring
against established institutions.

MUGGERIDGE: I wouldn't deny at all that from the point of
view of the State he was subversive. I'm saying, though, that he
was subversive in the sense that all sound human beings are
subversive. He was subversive because of his own conscience and
not because of the political philosophy. What the State asked
Bunyan to do under the King was to stop preaching.

BEVAN: I didn't say it was a political philosophy and I admit at
once that the book does develop a momentum as a religious
tract, but I think that Bunyan intended it to be read differently.
Otherwise, why say in his address to the readers 'Do not play
with the outside of my dream'?

MUGGERIDGE: All holy men are subversive. St Augustine was a
subversive.

BEVAN: Quite frequently in that period, Mr Muggeridge, as you
know, people had to write pamphlets of social progress in a
religious guise.

MUGGERIDGE: Of course.

BEVAN: They had to do it. There was a double meaning....

MUGGERIDGE: Yes, but I do not think that in that beautiful
phrase that you've quoted, he meant 'Don't think this is really
about God and about being good, it's actually about the
National Health Service.'

BEVAN: Let me read some more in order to show how Christian
comes back over and over again to the economic problems of the

day. Mr Worldly-Wiseman says: 'Hear me, I am older than thou. Thou art like to meet in the way thou goest wearisomeness, painfulness, hunger, perils, nakedness, swords lie in dragon's darkness' and so on, and Christian replies, 'Why sir, this burden upon my back is more terrible to me than all these things which you have mentioned,' and then Worldly-Wiseman repeats, 'It has happened unto other weak men, whom, meddling with things too high for them, do suddenly fall into thy distractions.'

MUGGERIDGE: But, Mr Bevan, the meaning of that is as clear as day, and it's the exact opposite of what you're saying.

BEVAN: And it's precisely because, if that is what you mean by the meaning of the book, it's so obviously dull.

MUGGERIDGE: If Mr Bevan regards it as a tract on social progress I would agree with him entirely; it's a second-rate one. But to me it is an exquisite image of a human being struggling with the difficulties of life and the confusion of moral values.

BEVAN: But it does not move me, because I cannot conceivably imagine in terms of our knowledge of men and women today how anybody can be condemned to hell fire, for example. I don't believe that people who sin sometimes, because they can't help it, or because they've got the wrong parents, are necessarily going to be condemned to eternal damnation.

MUGGERIDGE: Well I think that's a 'red herring'. The point really is Christian's journey. The day-by-day struggle. The Hill of Difficulty, the Slough of Despond, the Delectable Mountains. All those things are exquisitely described.

BEVAN: But then his reward is eternal glory.

MUGGERIDGE: But that's just an image.

BEVAN: I cannot sympathize with individuals who are either going to earn eternal glory, or who are condemned to horrible torment for things over which they can have no control at all.

MUGGERIDGE: Because an imagery becomes obsolete, it's validity doesn't become obsolete, that's the point.

BEVAN: I still maintain he was in fact speaking about his own people. When they read him, when they read that wonderful direct description of a man with a burden on his back, they read it because they saw in it what they wanted to see, which was a protest against the actual conditions of their lives.

Alice in Wonderland

The Gryphon speaks

Jonathan Miller's production is based on the situation of a real little girl confronted with the absurd grown-up world of un-reality which she will have to enter when, shortly, she reaches puberty. He sees Lewis Carroll's *Alice* as one more sick Victorian cry in the night against the monstrous encroachment of adolescence on the purity and innocence of childhood. Project it a little further and you get to Barrie and *Peter Pan*, a little further still and you get to Nabokov and *Lolita*. For Barrie the first drops of menstrual blood were all too terribly an intimation of mortality, the first leaden raindrops before a violent thunderstorm.

The reference to *Lolita* may seem far-fetched, but not after looking through the Rev. Charles Dodgson's collection of photographs, a selection of which were published in 1949,

edited with an interesting introduction by Mr Helmut Gernsheim. The photographs are nearly all of little girls in various conditions of undress; 'I wish,' Dodgson wrote to the *Punch* artist Harry Furniss, 'I dared dispense with *all* costume. Naked children are so perfectly pure and lovely; but Mrs Grundy would be furious – it would never do.' Children for him meant little girls – 'I confess I do *not* admire naked boys. They always seem to me to need clothes – whereas one hardly sees why the lovely forms of girls should ever be covered up.' Humbert Humbert would have understood perfectly. Sometimes parents did not object, and then Mrs Grundy could be ignored, though 'if I had the loveliest child in the world, to draw or photograph, and found she had a modest shrinking (however slight, and however easily overcome) from being taken nude, I should feel it was a solemn duty owed to God to drop the request *altogether*'.

It is highly characteristic of our time that Miller's transference of *Alice's Adventures in Wonderland* from the sick mind of Lewis Carroll to the sane mind of Alice herself should seem to imply the vicious travesty of an enchanting children's tale. *Alice* might conceivably bore juvenile viewers of all ages, it could not possibly shock them. This apart from any consideration as to whether children reared on *Batman* and occasional glimpses of adult favourites like *Peyton Place* and *The Man from UNCLE* are in fact shockable at all. *Alice* has long been part of contemporary folklore, and Miller's version, giving it a new, significant twist, necessarily becomes a piece of social history.

Veteran Humorist

A conversation with P. G. Wodehouse

Hilaire Belloc called him the greatest prose writer of our time. Evelyn Waugh acknowledged him as a master. In his eighties P. G. Wodehouse is still hard at it. Bertie Wooster and his gentleman's gentleman, Jeeves, take their place along with Don Quixote and Sancho Panza. Wodehouse lives now in seclusion in one of the remoter parts of Long Island some eighty miles from New York. He's become an American. Some broadcasts that he inadvertently delivered in Berlin during the War damaged his reputation for a time among his fellow-countrymen without, however, diminishing the number of Wodehouse addicts or the pleasures of their addiction.

MUGGERIDGE: Plummy, when were you last in England?

WODEHOUSE: Well, I actually came over for one day to see a cricket match in 1939, but apart from that I haven't been over since 1934.

MUGGERIDGE: Do you have a picture of England as it is now?

WODEHOUSE: Well I wonder, has it altered? Of course I get all the English papers. It doesn't sound as if it has altered so tremendously.

MUGGERIDGE: I don't know whether the old Drones Club would be quite as flourishing.

WODEHOUSE: No, I suppose everybody's got a job now.

MUGGERIDGE: The great thing about Bertie Wooster, as I recall, is that he never had anything particular to do, did he?

WODEHOUSE: Oh no, Bertie never did, no, he didn't do a stroke.

MUGGERIDGE: I think now he'd have to get a job in advertising or something, don't you think so?

WODEHOUSE: He'd have to get a job I think, oh yes.

MUGGERIDGE: Of course, in Jeeves you have created the most famous butler in the history of the world. Among your own acquaintances have you known many butlers?

WODEHOUSE: Well, I've had a lot of butlers. I must say they

were never anything like Jeeves.

MUGGERIDGE: What were your butlers like?

WODEHOUSE: Well, one of them – I forget which one it was, during the twenties – was jugged for robbery with violence, and he got about three years.

MUGGERIDGE: Jeeves has never been such a fool as to let himself be caught.

WODEHOUSE: No, Jeeves never would.

MUGGERIDGE: What do you feel about humorous writing to-day?

WODEHOUSE: It's rather depressing the way humour has died out. I mean, all the humour you get nowadays seems to be that vicious humour, you know; Lennie Bruce sort of stuff.

MUGGERIDGE: Anyway your books go on selling, don't they?

WODEHOUSE: The extraordinary thing is foreign countries seem to like them. The Swedes have always been very faithful.

MUGGERIDGE: Wodehouse standbys.

WODEHOUSE: But Italy and Germany and France and all that. What do the Japanese make of it, do you think?

MUGGERIDGE: I've got a certain slight theory about it. I think that people have a certain image of a country, and they like to have that image fulfilled.

WODEHOUSE: Yes.

MUGGERIDGE: And your image is what they would like to think England was, in fact isn't, and in a sense never was. How far were you consciously satirical?

WODEHOUSE: Oh, not at all.

MUGGERIDGE: I feel you are.

WODEHOUSE: I don't like satire at all.

MUGGERIDGE: But in your picture of life there is a satirical theme.

WODEHOUSE: I suppose in a way – sort of exaggerating certain traits, but I don't know.

MUGGERIDGE: In the war one of the German agents was dropped in England, and he was wearing spats. I love the idea of German Military Intelligence having read Wodehouse, and deducing that the way to pass as a native in England is to wear spats. This man landed, and was immediately arrested.

WODEHOUSE: Did you ever wear spats?

MUGGERIDGE: I never wore spats.

WODEHOUSE: I did.

MUGGERIDGE: You actually wore them?

WODEHOUSE: Oh rather. I used to put on my frock coat and my brother's top hat and my spats and I was set for my afternoon call.

MUGGERIDGE: You were in a bank for a time. I can't think how you managed there.

WODEHOUSE: I was the worst bank clerk there's ever been, I should think. I knew nothing about it. I couldn't make out what the thing was about at all.

MUGGERIDGE: But even then you used to write?

WODEHOUSE: Oh yes, I wrote frightfully hard in those days. I used to go back to my lodgings and write in the evenings and at night.

MUGGERIDGE: When did the thought first occur to you that you were going to be a writer?

WODEHOUSE: They tell me I was writing when I was five, but it seems rather extraordinary, doesn't it?

MUGGERIDGE: What is your life like now? Tell us your day. What time do you wake up?

WODEHOUSE: They're all exactly the same. I wake up at about eight, and then I do about three-quarters of an hour's exercise, and shave and have a bath and everything, have breakfast, and then I start work which I have to knock off at twelve because I want to see a television show called 'Love of Life', which ruins my morning's work. Then lunch. Then I take the dogs for a walk. We've got a dachshund and a boxer now, and I have to take them for a walk; and then I work again until about five, I have a cocktail, dinner – very early dinner for the sake of the help, and I generally read most of the rest of the evening. It sounds awfully dull and yet it isn't.

MUGGERIDGE: How many words do you reckon to write a day?

WODEHOUSE: Oh, I'm slowing up terribly. I used to be able to do a couple of thousand every day. Now I think I'm lucky if I do six hundred.

MUGGERIDGE: Do you revise?

WODEHOUSE: I'm always revising. I'm always re-reading the stuff and spotting a place where it needs another paragraph or another scene or something.

MUGGERIDGE: It's incredible to me. You've been writing every day, for years and years, in all circumstances?

WODEHOUSE: Yes.

MUGGERIDGE: Even in your German prison camp?

WODEHOUSE: Oh, rather, I wrote awfully well there. But I never got more than about three hundred words a day done.

MUGGERIDGE: How did you actually do it?

WODEHOUSE: Well, I was able to hire a German typewriter but I couldn't compose on it. I used to write by hand, very laboriously, and in a room with about fifty people playing ping-pong and singing and so on.

MUGGERIDGE: Were the German guards interested in it?

WODEHOUSE: Oh, they were very interested. They used to stand behind me watching me do it.

MUGGERIDGE: When you look back now to that ridiculous row in the war – about the broadcasts in Berlin – is it a painful memory?

WODEHOUSE: No, it isn't really. I wish it hadn't happened, of course, but I don't worry about it much now.

MUGGERIDGE: Do you feel any resentment about it?

WODEHOUSE: None whatever. No, I made an ass of myself and had to pay for it.

MUGGERIDGE: I mean nobody is unpleasant about it any more?

WODEHOUSE: Nobody writes to me, and nobody I meet is. I don't know what they are like in England.

MUGGERIDGE: I know on your birthday it was fantastic. Personally I think there was quite a bit of guilt feeling too.

WODEHOUSE: Oh yes.

MUGGERIDGE: What happens I think in these rows – and I was involved in a somewhat comparable one – is that very few people have actually read what the row is about.

WODEHOUSE: Exactly.

MUGGERIDGE: Do you read much contemporary writing?

WODEHOUSE: Not very much, no.

MUGGERIDGE: What books do you read with most pleasure?

WODEHOUSE: I'm afraid mystery stories nearly always. I've got an encyclopaedic knowledge of thrillers.

MUGGERIDGE: You know such a terrific lot about Shakespeare too. Do you still read Shakespeare?

WODEHOUSE: Oh I do. Now Shakespeare I do re-read regularly

about once a year.

MUGGERIDGE: The whole lot?

WODEHOUSE: Yes. How bad some of it is, isn't it?

MUGGERIDGE: Are you in any way interested in religion? That's another side of human beings.

WODEHOUSE: I'm not in the least, no.

MUGGERIDGE: Have you ever been at all religious?

WODEHOUSE: No. I never passed through that phase. They always say that when you are about fifteen or sixteen you pass through a religious phase, but I never did that.

MUGGERIDGE: You wouldn't object to Christianity, for instance.

WODEHOUSE: Oh no. I've definite views on what one's supposed to do in this world. I think you're supposed to bide by your conscience, and not hurt other people and so on, but I certainly wouldn't call myself a religious man.

MUGGERIDGE: What do you think about the after life, then?

WODEHOUSE: Well I rather lean to the spiritualistic idea. I think there is an awful lot in that.

MUGGERIDGE: What, you mean that people are still around?

WODEHOUSE: Yes.

MUGGERIDGE: That they communicate?

WODEHOUSE: Yes, I think so. There seems to be so much evidence for it. But I really don't know anything about anything in that line. I'm just hopeful.

MUGGERIDGE: Would it worry you if you knew that when you died, that was the complete and total end of you?

WODEHOUSE: Oh no, not in the least.

MUGGERIDGE: Have you ever suffered from boredom at all?

WODEHOUSE: Never. Now that is rather remarkable. I can't remember a time when I was bored.

MUGGERIDGE: Were your school days happy?

WODEHOUSE: Awfully. That seems very unfashionable now, doesn't it?

MUGGERIDGE: I think it's marvellous. I think that a man like you who has work that he likes doing, that he does incomparably well, and finds the circumstance of human life delightful, and is not bored, is a very fortunate man.

WODEHOUSE: Oh, I've always been very lucky....

Marriage

I think the interest of marriage and its pleasure is that it is
perpetually having to be sorted out.

Winter in Moscow

The story of a lost dream

In February 1934, my wife's aunt, Beatrice Webb – Fabian and fulsome apologist for Stalin's Russia – referred to me in her diary:

> 'In a little note of regret about my illness Malcolm wrote that he was "angry and bitter at the whole business of Soviet Russia". In a friendly answer I asked him why.

And my reply:

> 'Bitter and angry, Aunt Bo, because something I believed in has turned out to be a fraud. And now there's nothing to believe in. The most encouraging thing I found in the Soviet regime was its failure. If it had succeeded, I think I should have committed suicide, because then I should have known that there were no limits to the extent to which human beings could be terrorized and enslaved. I won't send you my novel *Winter in Moscow* because I know you'll hate it. It's an outpouring of anger and bitterness, in a way, futile.'

The England I turned my back on in 1932 was a dismal place. Old Jerusalem was falling down and no new one was rising in its place. From the *Manchester Guardian* office, resounding with Liberalism's dying platitudes, I gazed disconsolately out upon the ravages of what the politicians called an economic blizzard. It seemed to me evident beyond any shadow of doubt that capitalism, as Marx had foretold, was now irretrievably moribund and doomed – offering its captive workers no hope.

The militants took to the streets confidently supposing themselves to be the spearhead of a proletarian army. They – like me – fastened their eyes on the triumphant proletariat in Russia.

There at least, we believed, the Internationale really did unite the human race. This was the Marxist paradise which I was now to report for the blameless readers of the *Manchester Guardian*. In Russia I expected to find a perfect society created by Lenin's October Revolution. This was the dream I had.

What I actually found was chicanery, brutality and dictatorship. I poured out my bitter disappointment in a satirical novel, *Winter in Moscow*. The characters are all real people, many of them English, connected with the Soviet scene and easily recognizable by those in the know. Heaven knows what libel actions might have been brought!

In the book there is a Mr Aarons, a Soviet Foreign Office official who looked after distinguished visiting foreigners. One of these is Mrs Eardley Wheatsheaf digesting her notes in a corner. 'It all looked very well,' she thought. As a member of the LCC she'd often visited public institutions but she'd never investigated anything that for size and general excellence approached Mr Aaron's interesting Soviet Union.

Then there was Mrs Trivett. Bare, pink legs swelling out of tweed skirt, heavy breasts quivering, pale blue eyes lost in a pale vague face. 'Oh, Mr Aarons,' she said breathlessly, 'can you tell me about abortions? They're free, aren't they?'

The hero of the novel, a hero of sorts, was a certain Wraithby, a disillusioned English journalist – of course, me. In my early days in Moscow I used to spend a lot of time just walking the streets. The unending stream of people, grey-faced, anonymously clothed, had a curious attraction. This is how Wraithby saw them:

'They seemed to be going nowhere in particular, to have no particular object in view. There was little in the shop windows to look at and they did not, like crowds in other cities, take stock of one another: inscrutable, drifting along without any evident expectation of better times or fear of worse ones. There the world we were to live in, for good or ill, was being shaped. That noiseless, aimless procession through the blank houses was mankind processing through the twentieth century.'

I joined the little company of foreign journalists in Moscow.

Our impossible task was to find news when there were only handouts and lies, to report what we weren't permitted to see, and to explain what was inexplicable.

Foreign currency – *valuta* – was the password to the privileges we enjoyed – valid only in Torgsin shops where foreign delicacies, inconceivable luxuries, were on sale. Those of us with families set up house, usually in dachas outside the city. My wife Kitty and I found a perch in the suburb of Kliasma.

KITTY: I remember living at Kliasma. We loved that – much better than living in Moscow.
MUGGERIDGE: It was an old house and I loved it because as a lover of Russian novels it had this stove where the servants used to sleep.
KITTY: I went shopping in the market at the Torgsin, of course, with special vouchers. But it was always rather embarrassing, buying a lot of food and taking it back past people who hadn't got anything.
MUGGERIDGE: Do you remember how when we went to a restaurant the waiter would always come and whisper in one's ear, 'Rouble or valuta?' And if you said 'Rouble' he lost interest.

The big story when I arrived in Russia was the first Five-Year Plan. Stalin with the Supreme Economic Council presided over the shaping and execution of the Plan like God in Genesis over the creation of the world. The Plan laid down what was to be produced, where, and how much, in every department of life from tractors to hot-water bottles. Stalin's obsession was with heavy industry. In the new Soviet theology the turbines which continually do turn replaced cherubim and seraphim.

At the theatre the plays we saw had names like Cement and Slag. Painters called their sentimental landscapes 'From a Factory Window'. Even at the Moscow Races a horse called 'Pyatilyetka' – 'Five-Year Plan' – was a dead cert.

Man as producer, Man as consumer – I could hear the familiar Webbian duet intoned by Beatrice and Sidney over toast and a bright Hampshire log fire.

It was a cult of statistics to the greater glory of Stalin and his Proletariat. The newspapers were full of stories of heroic workers who pushed manganese production up to unprecedented levels. As percentages soared to ever dizzier heights, available supplies dwindled ever more abysmally.

Under the Plan the peasants were to provide food for the factory workers, but the produce they took to market only earned them useless roubles, for there was nothing to buy. So they humanly ate what they grew and the food queues in the cities grew longer. Stalin's characteristic response was to collectivize the farms by order and administer them by force.

The peasants in their turn slaughtered their cattle and ate the seed corn. With calculating callousness, Stalin launched a programme of liquidation of the kulaks – the richer peasants – and directed the resentment of the poorer ones against them. The famished countryside became a place of terror. Stalin made war on the peasants. The military were called in and resistance was put down with brutal coercion. The populations of entire villages were deported leaving them empty and deserted, as I saw for myself in the Ukraine and the Caucasus. Hundreds of thousands were herded like cattle to corrective labour in Siberia and the Arctic North.

It was a desolating spectacle, this wanton sacrifice of millions of lives for an idea. Stalin's collective farming turned some of the richest wheatlands in Europe into a wilderness.

Through this wilderness we journalists were taken by a special train to visit Dnieperstroi Dam. It was the journey I remember, not the dam. It was, I recall, a jolly affair. Someone brought along a gramophone. The railway carriage was a haven of rest and good cheer. Outside there were unspeakable horrors. 'I don't know what you're worrying about,' said the man from the Soviet Foreign Office, 'you've got plenty to drink.' We had.

Most of the stations had been cleared for our passage, but occasionally there would be a little huddled group of mujiks. At one station a German correspondent threw out a chicken leg he had been gnawing. The mujiks hurled themselves upon it. It was one of those little quick scenes which live with one like stigmata. In *Winter in Moscow* I wrote:

'Whatever else I may do or think in the future, he thought, I must never pretend that I haven't seen this. Ideas will come and go; but this is more than an idea. It is peasants kneeling

down and asking for bread. Something I have seen and understood.'

'The cinema,' Lenin said, 'is our greatest art,' and his followers
were McLuhanites before McLuhan. The medium was the
message and the message was the Party Line. The great Russian
film-makers such as Eisenstein doubled as Party hacks. Other
forms of art too were casualties of the class war. 'Art is dead,' it
was proclaimed. 'The new art must serve the new class, the
proletariat, its only function to further the task of Revolution.'
Official artists gave Stalin an imagined place beside Lenin. How
closely, I reflected, those innumerable portraits of Lenin and
Stalin resemble the Mayors and Aldermen, in leaden oils, to be
seen in any Town Hall.

Written history likewise followed, as it still does, the Party
Line. The sychophancy of Soviet scholarship touched depths
unknown even in Oxford and Cambridge. Writers, said Stalin,
were 'human engineers'. As such they clocked in, following a
decree of the Union of Soviet writers which laid it down that
'book production can be planned in advance, like the production of textiles and steel'. Sadly, even old Gorki gave his blessing
– I hoped a senile one – to this masquerade.

The actualities of Soviet life depressed me more and more.
Where I had looked to find a new and better society, I found a
new and better method of enslavement. The Bourbon kings
claimed, 'L'état c'est moi.' Stalin went further, 'Le people c'est
moi.' But the people he symbolized stood cowed in the background. It was only the élite, the Apparatchiks, who basked in
their leader's favour. To them he might be Little Father – to the
rest he was Big Brother. And when he opened his mouth all the
Communist dogs barked.

Every thought in every mind, whatever was spoken, written,
shouted, whispered – all subjected to the same centralized control. It was shattering, the more so because it gave every
appearance of working. Nothing else worked – not industry, not
agriculture, not the administration, but this did.

It was a new way of governing in an era of mass communications and technology, and as such bound to be copied everywhere – as it has been – by demagogues and advertisers as well
as by aspiring and actual dictators.

Even with Big Brother ever vigilant things still went wrong. Why? Sabotage of course! If weeds choked the good grain it could only be because someone had deliberately planted them. Who? Without any question, traitors anxious to deprive the triumphant proletariat of their food. Likewise, if production lagged it could only be because of sabotage by Russian or foreign engineers.

At the great show trials the accused, many of them the Revolution's founding fathers, publicly confessed to crimes they could not possibly have committed. Their real crime was that deep inside them they had disagreed with Stalin. Their fantastic confessions, as Koestler has so brilliantly shown, were in this sense genuine. The trials, in other words, were Morality Plays, part of the mysticism of power.

In Lubianka Prison in Moscow the GPU dealt with these class enemies, with the scapegoats of collectivization and the Five-Year Plan. I noticed how people in the street quickened their step and dropped their voices as they passed within its shadow.

But there were no doubts in the minds of the tourists who were now coming to Russia in increasing numbers. For the most part they were intellectuals of the Left, Privy Councillors to be, contributors to the *New Statesman* – the flower of our Western intelligentsia.

Intourist took them under its wing from the moment they disembarked at Leningrad and never thereafter let them out of its sight. They arrived in Moscow resolved to see what they had come to see and to hear what they had come to hear, their faith in the régime and in the Intourist guides who expounded it was unshakeable.

I can hear them now in their eager high-pitched voices, explaining away privations they would never have to endure and oppression that would never reach them. You can't make an omelette without cracking eggs, Walter Duranty, *New York Times* Correspondent, was fond of remarking after his umpteenth scotch. Omelette eaters of the world unite!

As I came to grasp their almost inconceivable credulity and näiveté, their readiness to believe anything, however absurd, that fitted in with their preconceived notions of this fairyland, I developed a contempt for them and their like which has stayed with me ever since.

Trades Union visitors were usually slightly more sceptical. They knew that by no stretch of the imagination could Transport House be built in Russia's green and pleasant land. Publicly, however, they were appropriately fraternal.

The most publicized and certainly the most fatuous of all the visitors to the USSR was, alas, Bernard Shaw, who came with Lady Astor in his train:

SHAW: ... Russia, her people employed to the last man and woman, her scientific agriculture doubling and trebling her harvest, her roaring and multiplying factories, her efficient rulers, her atmosphere of such hope and security as has never been seen before in a civilized country on earth.

Even more welcome were Beatrice and Sidney Webb, whose book *Soviet Communism: a New Civilization* had been checked, they proudly told me, page by page, by the Soviet Ambassador, Mr Maisky. 'In Russia,' Aunt Bo told me one day as we were striding along together over Hampshire shrubland, 'Sidney and I are icons now.'

Certainly the old icons seemed to have had their day. The Christian religion really was to wither away, its buildings desecrated, its treasures removed and its faithful dispersed. The Father, Son and Holy Ghost had been replaced by a new and unholy trinity: Lenin, Engels and Marx.

The new State Religion of progress and materialism did not lack for temples. Old Moscow was pulled down to make room for pretentious edifices in Stalinist Baroque.

Thus was my promised land being constructed with its many mansions rising hideously into the sky – a jerry-built immensity made and inhabited by slaves. Those great blocks of flats – were they not broiler houses controlled, conditioned, overshadowed by the sinister powers which had brought them to pass? A dreadful portent, as I considered, of what the twentieth century held in store.

All the hopes that brought me to Moscow became angry dust.

'The future seemed empty to Wraithby. It was easy to burn up

the past, but not so easy to face a future lacking everything
that had given that past substance. Even for him – a person of
no importance, a nobody – the patterns he'd made and un-
made in his mind had meant something. He knew that he had
reached an epoch in his life. There were two alternatives;
clearly marked; unmistakeable; and he had to choose between
them. It was a vision of Good and Evil, Heaven and Hell,
Life and Death. There were two alternatives and he had to
choose. He chose.'

And so I made off, with still ringing in my ears the insensate
adulation Stalin demanded from his own captive people and
was freely accorded by what passed as being the most enlightened, perceptive and humane minds of the Western world.

Looking back now across more than three decades, I see those
months I spent in the USSR, in a different light. The disil-
lusionment, such as it was, merges into a general sense that
power must invariably bring out the worst in those who exercise
it, and that the dream of a more humane and just and joyous
collective existence, whether entertained by a St Francis or a
Karl Marx or Philadelphia Founding Father, belongs – as the
psalmist puts it – to a land that is very far off.

There is also the land that is very near – I mean our earth
itself and all its creatures – conveying, for those that have eyes
to see, the image of another Paradise at once infinitely near and
infinitely distant; all Eternity in a grain of sand. *Winter in
Moscow* ends with Wraithby turning to this other Paradise.

'Suddenly Wraithby noticed a change in the wind that was
blowing against his face. It was touched with warmth. It was
fragrant. Suddenly spring had begun. The frozen river would
thaw, and the sun make the earth bare; then green. Thus it
had happened a million times before. Thus it would happen a
million times again. Nothing could prevent this process taking place – the sudden, unexpected coming of spring.'

Let Me Speak

Empire Loyalists endeavour to explain themselves

MUGGERIDGE: One may wonder how, since the British Empire patently no longer exists, it's possible to be loyal to it. Can one be loyal to a defunct Empire, or have perhaps these young Loyalists transferred their allegiance to the British Commonwealth? Is it now Mr Jomo Kenyatta, Dr Nkrumah and Dr Banda, who fire their blood? Somehow, I doubt it. But let's see.

MALE LOYALIST: We see no reason to change our prior title because of the aberrations of successive socialist and conservative administrators.

MUGGERIDGE: I don't think you quite understood my question. Can one be loyal to something which is no longer in existence?

MALE LOYALIST: The British Empire still exists. It may be not under its former title, but a spirit of unity still remains between the British nations. I mean Canada, Australia, New Zealand, and indeed Southern Rhodesia.

MUGGERIDGE: But you see, when you for instance say that the Conservatives and the Labour party have equally betrayed this Empire, I don't think you'd find many people in Canada or Australia to agree with you.

FEMALE LOYALIST: They perhaps disapprove of our methods or some of the things, but on the whole they feel that they are being sold out by white politicians; and this is what we feel too.

MUGGERIDGE: Isn't it curious that they return governments by the ordinary operation of Parliamentary domocracy which participate in these processes of what you call 'betraying the heritage of the white man'? Isn't that curious, or do you think that democracy itself is a fraud?

FEMALE LOYALIST: I think democracy is impossible.

MUGGERIDGE: But then what sort of government do you want to have?

FEMALE LOYALIST: I think a monarchy is a fine thing, it's a fine institution, about the safest one you can ever achieve.

MUGGERIDGE: But you mean a monarchy in which the monarch exercises power?

FEMALE LOYALIST: Yes, a monarchy, when the Queen is not the figurehead of politicians who use her as a tool, but when the Queen or the King has real power.

MUGGERIDGE: Then what you would like really would be for the Queen to rule us?

FEMALE LOYALIST: Yes to *rule* us, not to be a puppet.

MALE LOYALIST: We have no opinions as a League about the internal political structure of our country. We are concerned with the fall from grace of Great Britain; her decline from greatness.

MUGGERIDGE: Yes, but would you say that was entirely due to politicians, or do you think perhaps two world wars have been a factor in producing that result?

MALE LOYALIST: Mainly due to the lack of spirit of governments acting under duress from the American Government.

MUGGERIDGE: Do you mean that, if we had not been subservient to America, we would today, despite two world wars, despite nuclear weapons, all those things, exercise as much power in the world as we ever did?

MALE LOYALIST: We wouldn't be the football of fate, as we are at the moment.

MUGGERIDGE: But those are phrases, my boy, they are phrases. The point is there's such a thing as power, and power is represented by wealth and weapons.

MALE LOYALIST: That's precisely why we want to maintain our links with British people throughout the world. So there's no question of our standing alone.

MUGGERIDGE: But look at facts today, as they are. There are ten million, eleven million Australians far away in the Antipodes, on the fringe of an enormous continent, with a thousand million Asians round them.

FEMALE LOYALIST: I bitterly resent the implication they should welcome Asian immigration –

MALE LOYALIST: Yes, indeed –

MUGGERIDGE: All right – bitterly resent it – possibly recklessly – but bitterly resent it. Now, how if there is an atomic war are those people going to be defended? Do you imagine there's anything that we could produce here that would enable us to defend them?

MALE LOYALIST: We've got the V-bombers, what do you think they are for?

MUGGERIDGE: Do you want to break the American alliance?

FEMALE LOYALIST: Yes, yes.

MALE LOYALIST: No – no.

MUGGERIDGE: There you are.

MALE LOYALIST: Mr Muggeridge, it so happens that at this very moment Indonesians are being trained in the United States to attack Malaysia.

MUGGERIDGE: Come on, tell us how you know that?

MALE LOYALIST: It's been reported in *Human Events*.

MUGGERIDGE: A magazine that I happen to know.

MALE LOYALIST: If you took the trouble to read it you'd learn a great deal from it –

MUGGERIDGE: Well now, let's move on. What about your methods, what about the methods that you employ in order to promote your ideas? I was the recipient of some of the attentions of your organization at one time.

MALE LOYALIST: In which case you probably know how effective our methods are?

MUGGERIDGE: Yes I do. You came down to my house, or at least some of you did –

MALE LOYALIST: We don't want to hear this story –

MUGGERIDGE: I just wondered what you hoped to achieve by doing things like that, that's all.

MALE LOYALIST: Well it seems to have worried you.

MUGGERIDGE: Not at all, I was glad to have the opportunity of making the acquaintance of some of you.

MALE LOYALIST: We, Mr Muggeridge, reserve the right to bring our case before the public by making peaceful demonstrations.

MUGGERIDGE: What do you call a peaceful demonstration?

FEMALE LOYALIST: We have never once offered violence. No, we have once offered violence, when an old man slapped a much younger man than yourself in the face for insulting the Monarchy.

MALE LOYALIST: As indeed you did, Mr Muggeridge, if you remember, in a foreign magazine.

MUGGERIDGE: I expressed in a magazine –

FEMALE LOYALIST: Cheap personal remarks –

MUGGERIDGE: Certain ideas that I had –

FEMALE LOYALIST: Cheap personal remarks –

MUGGERIDGE: Now you don't of course know what's meant by freedom, but that's what freedom means.

FEMALE LOYALIST: But, Mr Muggeridge, we don't insult people that by virtue of their position cannot hit back, such as the Queen.

MUGGERIDGE: The Monarchy is a public office.

MALE LOYALIST: Not the Monarchy, Mr Muggeridge, but the Queen –

MUGGERIDGE: I was talking about the Monarchy, and the Monarchy is a public office, and as a public office every free citizen is fully entitled to express his opinions about it. If you don't understand that, then you don't understand what a free society is. And if you think that by shouting and scrawling things on people's houses and so on, you're making a point, that's where you're mistaken. There's only one way to make a point, and that is by argument.

MALE LOYALIST: A dirty cheap article.

MUGGERIDGE: That's your opinion, that's your opinion –

MALE LOYALIST: It's general opinion –

MUGGERIDGE: I simply say that as a free citizen of a free country I enjoy the right to express what opinions I hold about anything. And if people like you ever get into power, this is precisely what would come to an end.

FEMALE LOYALIST: But we say nothing but the truth, Mr Muggeridge.

MUGGERIDGE: Well, I think the way you behave –

MALE LOYALIST: We behave!

MUGGERIDGE: – suggests to me that your sympathies lie with people who have used violence to express –

MALE LOYALIST: Such as whom?

MUGGERIDGE: Such as Fascists.

MALE LOYALIST: Well-known smear, we might have expected that –

MUGGERIDGE: You have no sympathy with them?

FEMALE LOYALIST: None . . .

MUGGERIDGE: Nor their leaders?

MALE LOYALIST: No – none whatsoever.

MUGGERIDGE: Are you racialists?

MALE LOYALIST: What do you mean by that?

MUGGERIDGE: What I mean by racialism is the insistence on the superior rights of one race over another, as is happening for instance in South Africa. Three million people saying that for all eternity we must be dominant over ten million people. That's racialism. Do you agree with that?

MALE LOYALIST: It is simply the maintenance of a civilized government as opposed to the Congo.

MUGGERIDGE: So that you are saying that it is right that three million people must for all time –

MALE LOYALST: It's unavoidable, there's no question of right or wrong –

MUGGERIDGE: I take the position that it is inconceivable historically that three million people should for ever hold dominance over ten million.

MALE LOYALIST: What about what is happening to the white people in Kenya and Ghana and other parts of Africa, and Belgian women in the Congo. Is that what you would like?

FEMALE LOYALIST: I suppose you would agree that the white people had no right to suppress Mau Mau, because Mau Mau was the majority opinion.

MUGGERIDGE: I didn't say that white people had no right to suppress Mau Mau – I haven't even said what my views on South Africa are.

MALE LOYALIST: Mr Muggeridge, do you defend the tyranny in Ghana? Do you defend the harsh laws?

MUGGERIDGE: I don't defend, my boy, I –

MALE LOYALIST: This programme is called 'Let me Speak'. Why don't you let me speak?

MUGGERIDGE: I'd be delighted. I want to hear you –

MALE LOYALIST: I'm asking you a string of questions.

MUGGERIDGE: Right – ask your questions.

MALE LOYALIST: Do you agree with –

MUGGERIDGE: Ask me a question and I'll answer it.

MALE LOYALIST: D'you – why don't you let me get it out first.

MUGGERIDGE: Come on –

MALE LOYALIST: I'm trying my best.

MUGGERIDGE: Come on then – get it out.

MALE LOYALIST: Do you agree with the present policies of the

Government in Ghana which has suppressed liberty?

MUGGERIDGE: I don't agree with the suppression of liberty any-where or in any circumstances, in any community, and in so far as I have tried to pursue one idea throughout my life, it is that, to *hate* it wherever I find it. And wherever I find a group of young people like you, for whatever motives, being attracted by this idea of a few dominating many, because they are going to give them order and good government, I watch out.

MALE LOYALIST: Do you also attack the way Communist Russia has enslaved twelve great nations and about 84 million people?

MUGGERIDGE: If you took the trouble to look up newspaper cuttings and things that I've written, you'd find that there was probably nobody who had protested longer or more consistently against such things as that.

MALE LOYALIST: It's easy for you to speak, Mr Muggeridge, because if violence did come to South Africa you wouldn't suffer one iota, would you?

MUGGERIDGE: Nor did I suffer when the Hungarian Revolution took place, nor have I suffered in a great many cases in which violence has been done to a principle in which I believe. But that doesn't prevent me from protesting against them.

MALE LOYALIST: You're not going to suffer if stability and order and law does break down in South Africa, or anywhere else.

MUGGERIDGE: You have just characteristically made exactly the same point again.

MALE LOYALIST: You didn't understand it the first time.

MUGGERIDGE: I understand it perfectly! If you are saying that no man may uphold a principle unless he is directly involved in the consequences, then you would deny the right of people through the centuries to express their views about principles.

MALE LOYALIST: I'm not –

MUGGERIDGE: You are –

MALE LOYALIST: I'm simply questioning your judgement. But can we get back to Dr Nkrumah and Kenyatta, and various other –

MUGGERIDGE: I asked whether your loyalty to the empire ex-tended to the Commonwealth?

FEMALE LOYALIST: Our loyalty extends to the white people.

MUGGERIDGE: Not to the modern Commonwealth?

MALE LOYALIST: We accuse this government of treason in betraying the white people in Kenya to Kenyatta who is the manager of Mau Mau. You might remember that.

MUGGERIDGE: Now what would you have done about giving Kenya its independence, what would you have done about that?

MALE LOYALIST: Kenya is not ready for independence, and it never will be. I believe the white people have to rule.

MUGGERIDGE: And you think empires are desirable –

MALE LOYALIST: This one was in its time, and this one was betrayed before its time ended.

MUGGERIDGE: The ends of empires are chaos, they always have been.

MALE LOYALIST: There are bigger barbarians leading black Africa than there are in South Africa or Southern Rhodesia.

MUGGERIDGE: This might even be true, this might even be true.

MALE LOYALIST: Well, why do you want to subject these people to a tyranny of their own kind – black over black?

MUGGERIDGE: I'm trying to understand what's going on in the world and that's what you're not doing. You're reacting violently, and you're not trying to understand; you don't understand –

MALE LOYALIST: What do you mean – violently?

MUGGERIDGE: Well, by shouting.

MALE LOYALIST: Mr Muggeridge, today we see two empires in this world: the dollar empire and the Russian empire, and this is what's come through the split up of the British empire.

MUGGERIDGE: I'm trying to explain to you, if you could possibly understand but I'm afraid you can't, that it's not a question of approving of what goes on in the world; it's a question of recognizing what goes on in the world –

FEMALE LOYALIST: But we do recognize –

MUGGERIDGE: This is the approach that you're incapable of making, and that's why, although your movement is a completely derisory one, there's a grave danger in the sort of attitude of mind that you have.

MALE LOYALIST: But who derides it?

MUGGERIDGE: I do.

MALE LOYALIST: You do.

MUGGERIDGE: Yes.

MALE LOYALIST: I'd say people like you are a danger, personally.
(*All shouting together*)

Franchise

I think that the people who don't vote are the absolute flower of our community – they are the élite.

The only candidate I ever wanted to vote for was a man who based his appeal on the fact that, having been confined in a lunatic asylum, he had a certificate of sanity.

Lord Beaverbrook

No other newspaper proprietor, it's safe to say, not even North-cliffe, has stamped his product so indelibly with his own image. Yet in the very success with which he's fashioned an instrument for expounding and spreading his views lies the irony of his life, ostensibly so successful. Rarely, if ever, has so stentorian a voice been so little heeded. Lord Beaverbrook is by ancestry and by instinct an evangelist. He's fought the bad fight with all his might. It's difficult indeed to think of any cause advocated by him which has thriven. Or of any target of the various vendettas

conducted by his newspapers who had been seriously harmed thereby. He pronounces anathema, his mercenaries go into action, and lo, when the dust settles, the citadel is intact, the adversary unhurt.

Political Honours

After the Prime Minister's statement about Honours, throughout the Home Counties and beyond massive ladies in tweed suits and gardening gloves have been heard openly sobbing over their rose beds, and Lt.-Colonels with trimmed white moustaches groaning and howling as they mowed their lawns within sight of Sevenoaks station. No more OBEs and MBEs for party political services in the annual Queen's Birthday and New Year hand-outs. A cruel blow indeed!

There was a time not so very long ago in the good old Lloyd George days when honours and peerages were on free sale. A barony cost £40,000. A Viscountcy rather more – up to £100,000

– though, if Lord Beaverbrook is to be believed, Lord Astor paid twice that sum for his. And a knighthood could be picked up for as little as £10,000. A middle man in the business named Maundy Gregory got caught out and had to be prosecuted. After serving a short sentence he decamped to Paris where he lived quietly as Sir Arthur Gregory. It showed a becoming modesty on his part. There was, after all, nothing to stop him giving himself a peerage. When he ran short of money he just used to send postcards to former clients announcing his intention of returning to London. Cheques came rolling in by return of post.

A favourite anecdote of Gregory's was of a client who signed a cheque in payment for a peerage with the title he proposed to take, thus ensuring that there would be no double-dealing. Another case that he liked to dwell on was of an aspiring nobleman who paid for his peerage on the instalment plan and died before the payments were completed, thereby creating a problem for his heirs.

After Gregory a committee was set up to ensure that thenceforth peerages and other honours should be disinterestedly bestowed. This did not preclude the ennoblement of Lord Thomson of Fleet, who, according to his biographer, Russell Braddon, sent his nationalization papers to the office of the then Prime Minister, Mr Macmillan, marked 'For Attention'. He received them back marked 'Duly Noted', and was awarded his peerage in the next Honours List.

It seems extraordinary, in a way, that any sane citizen should still want to become a lord or a member of an Order named after an empire which no longer exists. Yet, as any Prime Minister's postbag clearly indicates, the appetite remains undiminished. This has its advantages. Honours and decorations cost nothing; if their recipients had to be bribed to keep in line it would become expensive. An American President, groaning over the spoils system, would be only too glad to have a few peerages and knighthoods to bestow. Dryden's line on a politician of the day – 'For almonds he'll cry whore to his own mother' – remains apposite if for almonds we read MBEs.

Heart Transplants

Extracts from two television programmes

(1) *From a discussion with Sir Henry Aitken, President of the Royal College of Surgeons, and Dr David Mendel, cardiologist.*

MUGGERIDGE: My feeling is a religious feeling. And therefore it is not completely rational. Rationally, you can argue that to regard a lately expired or just about to expire body as a collection of spare parts, available for other bodies, is a perfectly reasonable thing to do. But to me as a Christian it is deeply repugnant. What is more, I am absolutely convinced that the effect of taking such a view on others, in their whole attitude to the circumstances of their being, will be deplorable. Of course the Nazis went in for this sort of thing. They went in for a lot of experiments; they had plenty of spare parts. And, of course, as time goes on, you will find there will be plenty of spare parts. Sir Henry Aitken has already spoken about people who are living a cabbage existence. There might not be quite enough. Then there are a lot of people in lunatic asylums, and from a purely rational, medical view, those people should not live. Therefore, if their organs can be valuable, let us take them. May I make one last point, that struck me about this thing. You have there these twelve or fourteen highly trained doctors performing this operation which will enable middle-aged lives to be protracted a little further, on the edge of a continent in which in fact there are not for millions of fellow-human beings the minimal medical services available – not high-faluting things like grafting kidneys, but medicine, simple disinfectants...

AITKEN: Well, Mr Muggeridge, you're certainly correct in saying you take an emotional and not a rational view of this problem. I would say that to use emotive words such as Nazi and so on, in connection with an effort which the medical profession is making to promote happiness in the human race, is something which I really deplore and I think is something quite improper. But I would ask you one question. If you had a child whom you loved and that child's life could be saved by the implantation of a heart, would you allow it to be done?

MUGGERIDGE: I should be in an extremely difficult position. But if it were done in the circumstances in which the transplants have hitherto been done and will be done as far as the foreseeable future is concerned – no, I would be extremely, tragically unhappy. If I thought that my child was walking about with the heart of that coloured boy, that was taken off him, before they were absolutely certain he was dead, without his relatives having the faintest idea of what was happening, I would be tragically miserable.

MENDEL: I don't think there are any ethical problems of any major degree at all. I think ever since doctors started giving pills to patients, ever since they started giving blood transfusions to patients, there have always been people who've insisted that this is the beginning of the end, and that the patient would be better off dead, than with those awful chaps' blood inside them. And this is just another move in the same direction. We accept corneal grafting from dead people, we accept kidney grafting, and the heart is just the next thing on the list. There is no difference of kind in this. And in addition it's temporary, because it won't be very long before you can wait until the patient is actually dead, but incontrovertibly dead, and then you can store the organ.

MUGGERIDGE: What you leave out of account, I think, is that we who are uneasy about this – and it's not an uneasiness that's based on any hostility to doctors – we have a different idea of human life. An idea which does not, as Sir Henry does, assume that if you can manage by one means or another to add a few years to a man's life, you are making him happier ...

MENDEL: But this is a doctor's job. The doctor looks after the welfare of his patients, he looks after the welfare of the donor patient, and he looks after the welfare of the recipient. Your view is the view of the healthy man who sees nothing but a rosy future.

MUGGERIDGE: My view is of a man who for instance made a television programme about a pilgrimage to Lourdes and had to ask himself all the time whether those miserable people being transported to that place, whether it was worth while. They were useless mounds, they were cabbage people, a lot of them, and the conclusion that I reached was that there is another valuation of human beings than their physical well-being. And it is that valuation that I've fastened on to and stake my life on.

AITKEN: Mr Muggeridge, you and I are in absolute agreement over this. Life has both quantity and quality, and it is most important that the medical profession – and they do I'm sure – should realize the value of the spiritual aspect of life. I think that it is this they are pursuing in this exercise: that when all spiritual values of life have disappeared, when life no longer exists and cannot any longer exist, then this is not a person who can be insulted.

(2) *From a discussion with Professor Christian Barnard, Professor Calne, the Rev. Kenneth Slack, Lord Platt and Dr James Mowbray. Raymond Baxter in the chair.*

MUGGERIDGE: The Christian concept is that man is made in the image of God. From this, it seems to me to follow that man's body, like all creation, deserves our deep respect. Now the view of science, from which I admit the majority of people today get their moral concepts, such as they are, suggests that in fact man's physical necessities must take precedence over all others. And it is in following this notion, as I see it, that our human society is being transformed into a sort of vast broiler house or factory farm, such as satirists like Orwell and Aldous Huxley have envisaged.

RAYMOND BAXTER: Professor Barnard, are you turning us into a lot of broiler-house fowls?

MUGGERIDGE: Don't let that deflect you, Professor Barnard. You know the poet Blake said a robin redbreast in a cage puts high heaven in a rage. Now I wonder what the fury of heaven would be of the notion that our bodies are collections of spare parts.

BARNARD: I think Professor Calne would like to say something.

CALNE: I've got a picture that I would rather like to show. It's older even than Mr Muggeridge. (*Laughter.*)

MUGGERIDGE: I congratulate you.

CALNE: It's a painting of Fra Angelico, of the legends of Saint

Cosmos and Damien, doing a cadaver transplant of a leg, removed from somebody who had recently died, to a man dying from cancer of the leg. According to the legend, this was a complete success. Now this is an extremely important concept that goes back to the earliest of Christian thought. And I doubt if there is any serious religious objections to this type of principle of a dead person helping to save the life of somebody who is afflicted with a mortal disease.

BAXTER: And what a happy coincidence that you should happen to have the picture with you. (*Laughter.*)

BARNARD: I'm sorry I can't give you the exact text and verse, but the heart transplantation had been predicted in the Bible. It says that I will remove your heart of stone and replace it with a heart of flesh.

CALNE: The Devil said it ... (*Laughter.*)

MUGGERIDGE: This is something that I assure you is very genuinely felt. You're simply evading it by producing this picture by various devices.

SLACK: I do think that when Mr Muggeridge said he has this feeling, and many citizens have it, he is absolutely right.

MUGGERIDGE: Thank you.

SLACK: I am sure he is utterly wrong when he fathered it on to the Christian faith.

PLATT: Can I ask if Mr Muggeridge would refuse or accept a corneal transplant if he were blind and it was going to restore his sight, because surely this is exactly the same ...

MUGGERIDGE: No, it's not exactly the same, sir, with all respect. I would, under certain circumstances, accept an eye because I would know that it was removed from a body that was indubitably dead.

MOWBRAY: There is at least one transplant patient in this audience. Shouldn't they have a right to say what they think about it? Instead of us deciding whether they should be transplanted or not.

BAXTER: What is your reaction to Mr Muggeridge's attitude?

TRANSPLANT PATIENT: All I can say is I am very grateful for my spare parts.

BAXTER: And are you well?

PATIENT: Yes, perfectly well.

BAXTER: Can we know what the transplant is in the lady's case?

PATIENT: A kidney transplant.

MEDICAL STUDENT: I should like to ask Mr Muggeridge if he would accept a blood transfusion from a patient who was indubitably alive.

MUGGERIDGE: Not only would I accept it, I've given my blood and given it with the utmost satisfaction, given it with a sense of delight ... Almost everything I say makes these distinguished doctors laugh, it's very gratifying. (*Laughter.*) Very gratifying indeed.

Kipling Sahib

An illustrated lecture delivered to the Kipling Society

I remember very vividly, as though it were yesterday, strolling along the Mall in Simla around six o'clock on a November evening thirty-two years ago, and thinking suddenly of Rudyard Kipling with such intense vividness that it almost seemed he was there with me. If one had happened to believe in ghosts, I reflected, his presence in that place would have been in no way surprising. It was Anglo-India in excelsis, and he was the prophet, the chronicler, the poet of Anglo-India, the only one. If he were to walk anywhere, it would surely be there on just such an evening – the distant, majestic Himalayas glowing with the light of the setting sun, and the notes of *'Colonel Bogey'*, played by a military band in full regalia, sounding so clearly in the crystalline mountain air from the bandstand further along the Mall.

I, too, at that time was working on an Indian newspaper, as Kipling had some half century before. There, I may add, the resemblance ended. Few any longer believed in the Englishman's destiny to rule over palm and pine; least of all me. In the fifty years since Kipling's time the British Raj he extolled had grown tired and feeble, and was soon to come to an end in great bloodshed and ignominy. Yet if posterity ever cares to know about our short-lived conquest of India, one among so many, it is from Kipling's writings alone that they may learn what it was like: from the seeming magnificence of Viceregal power and glory down to Eurasian ticket-collectors, Babu clerks, and the urchin boy, offspring of a drunken Irish trooper who grew up amidst the dust and gossip and squalor of an Indian bazaar: Kim, the embodiment of all Kipling's first, fresh delight in the sights and sounds and vast diversity of that fantastic land and its diverse, fantastic people. We English have left behind no Taj Mahal to remind the world that once we ruled over India – only a few of our old haunts like Simla: hill stations, clubs, the grounds for polo players and other national idiosyncrasies. If the British Raj is remembered at all, it will be because of Kipling. Artistically speaking he is its single notable product and its only enduring memorial.

Kipling was born in Bombay on 30 December 1865. He spent but seven of his adult years there – 1882 to 1889. Yet, for me, his response to India represented far and away the deepest and most formative experience of all, at any rate as far as his writings were concerned. He positively looked like an Indian (the source of the ridiculous, but widespread rumour that he was really a Eurasian), being sallow and supple, and maturing early for an Anglo-Saxon. He had a moustache while still a schoolboy. If he had never been to India he would have been a totally different person. Perhaps some boring and pedantic don lost in the fastnesses of Eng. Lit., in which he was exceptionally well versed. Or, following a clear bent, one of those tedious maniacs about machines who insist on explaining to all and sundry how the wheels go round. India, it seems to me, in one premature exotic harvest brought out all that was most imaginative and warm and intuitive in him, and, at the same time, planted in him the proneness to adulate power and action – those two black sirens – which so often vulgarized his emotions and distorted his judgements.

It was this aspect of his character which Max Beerbohm found so offensive, and which induced him to draw a particularly cruel cartoon of Kipling. I spoke to Beerbohm about it in Rapallo a year or so before he died, and it visibly saddened him. He regretted the drawing's venom, he said, more particularly as Kipling had gone out of his way to be kind to him when he first began to write.

Still strolling along the Mall in Simla with that so vivid a sense of Kipling's presence upon me, I could project my life as it then was into his when he was working as a journalist in India. The very presses (rotary in my case, flatbed in his) seeming to make their mechanical movements languidly in the sweltering heat; the Indian proof-readers chanting uncomprehendingly the stilted sentences of the next day's paper, like weird priests; the curling galleys, so limp and damp and lifeless, black rivulets of ink spreading over them like the Hoogly's delta, when one made corrections; the punkahs waving to and fro in solemn uselessness, and the insects flying in dark clouds about the lamps, then falling, to pile up in high heaps of transparent holocausted dead. In such circumstances thinking was a slow, laborious business; words had to be laboriously extracted, and arranged with the studied deliberation of a drunk counting his change. Outside, there was the incredible Indian night, so fantastically rich in texture; full of little lights and distant tinkling sounds, and muffled chatter, and shuffling bare footsteps, and alternating whiffs of stench and fragrance which made one's heart stand still. With the paper put to bed, and the presses subsiding into stillness like a heart that stops beating, there was the Club to go to; a cavernous place, smelling of cheese and cold beef, where a few mildly tipsy Sahibs in cummerbunds and white coats tried to play billiards watched by inscrutable servants.

Kipling has made a hero, if not a god, of the upper-class Englishman, prototype of the Sahib, such as young George Cottar, the hero of his short story '*The Brushwood Boy*', who moves inevitably from public school to Sandhurst.

'His reward was another string of athletic cups, a good-conduct sword, and, at last, her Majesty's Commission as a subaltern in a first-class line regiment. He did not know that he bore with him from school and college a character worth much fine gold, but was pleased to find his mess so kindly. He had plenty of money of his own; his training had set the public-school mask upon his face, and had taught him how many were the "things no fellow can do". By virtue of the same training he kept his pores open and his mouth shut.'

This excessive adulation led Kipling into transports which now seem almost imbecile. When Cottar Sahib comes on his first home leave from India,

'the house took toll of him, with due regard to precedence – first the mother; then the father; then the housekeeper, who wept and praised God; and then the butler; and so on down to the under-keeper, who had been dog-boy in George's youth, and called him "Master George".'

Finally, his mother comes to tuck him up,

'and they talked for a long hour, as mother and son should, if there is to be any future for our Empire'.

It may be doubted, however, whether Kipling ever managed wholly to acclimatize himself to the Sahibs' India, much as he wanted to. English journalists in his day, even more than in mine, were, hierarchically speaking, of small account. At a Viceregal dinner their place was with the lowliest – among missionaries and even 'natives', as Kipling punctiliously calls Indians who are not so far above him in rank as to be princely, or so far below him as to be droll. The English in India soon followed the example of the Hindus they had conquered, and instituted their own caste system, in which everyone had his due place and status expressed in terms of his salary and the decorations which fell to him.

In Kipling's fragment of autobiography, *Something of My-self*, written in old age, he describes how one evening when he was a young man he was hissed in the Lahore Club. It was an incident which obviously made a deep impression on him. One can imagine how distressed Kipling must have been. He, the laureate of the Sahibs and their Raj, found himself in disfavour in their holy of holies, the Club, with Indian servants witnessing his discomfiture. Whenever the imaginatively gifted turn to glorifying authority, or its janus-face, revolution, they are liable to find themselves in such predicaments. Kipling's recourse was to fall back on the black mystique of action and violence. At the end of *The Light That Failed*, that truly atrocious novel, the hero, Dick Heldar, having gone blind, manages to make his way to the Sudan where he is fortunate enough to hear and smell slaughter before a stray bullet kills him. 'What luck!' he exclaimed. 'What stupendous and imperial luck ... Oh, God has been good to me!'

It was such glorifications of violence and sometimes cruelty in his writings (for Kipling in his life was affectionate, wonderful with children and kindly) which horrified the more squeamish among his contemporaries. When Andrew Lang was shown Kipling's story '*The Mark of the Beast*', written in 1890 before its author was known in England, he described it as 'poisonous stuff', and another – William Sharp – to whom the manuscript was referred recommended the instant burning of so detestable a piece of work, and predicted that the author would die mad before the age of thirty. One sees the point. In '*The Mark of the Beast*' an Indian leper is savagely tortured by two Sahibs, and there is unmistakable relish in the recounting of the episode.

After I returned to England from India in 1936, I went to live in Sussex, a few miles away from Burwash and Kipling's home Bateman's, where he settled in 1903, and spent the last thirty-three years of his life. He, who was by temperament as rootless as Kim, rooted himself with singular tenacity, if not ferocity, in this place, to which he belonged no more than I did. On my own restless walks in the locality, as on the Mall in Simla, I was somehow abnormally conscious of Kipling. There must have been something mediumistic about him which made his physical being extrude from his writings to an unusual, or even abnormal, degree. To me, at any rate, his spirit brooded palpably over that countryside which he so brilliantly evoked in his writings.

I recall an evening in early summer by the Rother, with the grazing cows seeming to be afloat on the mist rising over the lush meadowland, heavy with sodden pasture and creamy buttercups. There I saw him – a little, dark, spectacled man, so alien a figure, and yet pulling out of the scene its quintessence, his gaze behind the thick spectacle lenses digging deep into the land itself, and excavating out its history.

A portrait of Kipling, as I see it, should be in the medieval style, with a white angel perched on one shoulder and a black devil on the other. The white angel signifies the imagination, out of which come truth and love and laughter; the black devil signifies the will, out of which come rhetoric, hate and portentousness. Kipling was always, it seems to me, in the thrall to one or other of those two daemons. He found no peace in the quiet grey twilight between their two kingdoms where most of us reside. All writers are split personalities; literature is a current which flows between the two poles of mysticism and action. Kipling was an extreme case.

It is his memories of India which seem to stir most infallibly the imaginative side of him. Take the case of *'Without Benefit of Clergy'*. This marvellous story is about a love affair between a Sahib and an Indian girl who initially has been bought by him for money. Subsequently he falls in love with her, and she bears him a son. To the mother's and his infinite grief the child dies, and then the mother dies in a cholera epidemic, and the Sahib goes disconsolately away muttering to himself: 'Oh, you brute! You utter brute!' One may wonder why, in the circumstances, the Sahib's grief should take so self-condemnatory a form. Is it, I ask myself, because the story relates to some actual experience in Kipling's life? If this were so it might help to account for the curious fact that, though an inveterate traveller, Kipling visited India only once again, for a few days, after he left for England at the age of twenty-four.

Kipling himself managed to see some of the action he so admired in the South African War, when for the first time England came up against a tough opponent, after a series of easy victories against Tibetans, Zulus and other relatively speaking unarmed fuzzy-wuzzies. Prior to this Kipling's idea of war was largely based on the Indian North-West Frontier – a romantic, but not very dangerous style of fighting which, contrary to Sahib mystique, came to an abrupt end when India achieved independence. Though few recognized it at the time, least of all Kipling, the South African War marked the beginning of the decline of the British Empire, and of the cause of imperialism to which Kipling dedicated his life and work.

In South Africa Kipling made the acquaintance of Cecil Rhodes, and they became, in a manner of speaking, friends. They would sit together in silence for long periods of time, with Rhodes's huge body stretched out on a sofa; then, twisting and turning, he would ask: 'What am I trying to say, Ruddy?' Ruddy might well have retaliated by asking Rhodes: 'What am I trying to do?' They make, it seems to me, a perfect pair – the tubercular giant who became a millionaire on the diamond-fields before he was twenty, and the little short-sighted poet who became world-famous at about the same age.

'What's your dream?' was a question Rhodes was fond of putting. What was Kipling's dream, I wonder? It seems to me he was preoccupied with power in the same sort of way that D. H. Lawrence was preoccupied with sex. In India, when he was there, power was symbolized by the British Raj, and he bowed down before it. Yet in his masterpiece *Kim* the Lama, with his unworldly passion to escape from the Wheel of Life, is the dominant figure, and even Kim finds himself poised between his service to the Raj and to the Lama. Moreover Kipling's veneration for authority as such by no means extended to what we nowadays call the Establishment. He despised, with increasing bitterness, the conduct of affairs under his cousin Stanley Baldwin's premiership; his poem 'Gehazi', about Lord Reading, then Lord Chief Justice, is among the most scorching in the language:

> Stand up, stand up, Gehazi,
> Draw close thy robe and go,
> Gehazi, Judge in Israel,
> A leper white as snow.

He lived to see Gehazi-Reading become Viceroy of India, which must have given a great impetus to the mounting gloom about the prospects for England and the Empire which clouded his latter years. I see him at Bateman's when, as often happened, sleep eluded him, and, as he put it in *Something of Myself*, the night got into his head, shutting him out from the City of Sleep.

> Over the edge of the purple down,
> Where the single lamplight gleams,
> Know ye the road to Merciful Town
> That is hard by the Sea of Dreams –
> Where the poor may lay their wrongs away,
> And the sick may forget to weep?
> But we – pity us! Oh, pity us! –
> We wakeful; ah, pity us! –
> We must go back with Policeman Day –
> Back from the City of Sleep!

It has always seemed extraordinary to me that this strange fancy which Kipling, even as a young man, felt deeply should have been incorporated in a story as otherwise commonplace as 'The Brushwood Boy'. Yet there it is – the dream which came to the Brushwood Boy to solace him in moments of desolation when the breathless Indian night seemed to suffocate him; a dream more real than life, also dreamed in identical terms by the woman he was to marry before they had made each other's acquaintance. Their mutual recognition when they met in the flesh made them realize that love exists before it comes to pass and goes on existing after it is dead.

Kipling's death in 1936 coincided with King George V's. There was another less noticed death at the same time – that of Saklatvala, an Indian Parsee who had become the Communist MP for Battersea. It so happened, as I have read, that Kipling's cremation followed Saklatvala's, and at the crematorium there was no time to clear away the Red Flags and other Communist insignia set up for Saklatvala. Truly God is not mocked.

Tailor and Cutter

A sartorial dispute

MUGGERIDGE: I've got here tonight Mr John Taylor, who's the editor of the *Tailor and Cutter*, a very eminent journal, supreme in its field, and I'm going to ask him, if he'd be so kind, without being unduly insulting, to comment on my appearance.

TAYLOR: Well, as long as you have no solicitors secreted about you, Mr Muggeridge, I would say that the thing that mainly worries me about you is a sort of greyness that you present –

MUGGERIDGE: It's drab you think?

TAYLOR: No, not necessarily, but rather unimaginative – the grey shirt, the grey tie, the grey suit –

MUGGERIDGE: Shabby?

TAYLOR: No, no, no, but coupled with the grey hair and the grey eyebrows it's rather a formidable experience you know. The jacket is very nice, it's short, which of course is a fashionable thing, but I rather feel that you've had that one long enough for the fashion to come round again –

MUGGERIDGE: Mr Taylor, you're dead right – but that was no question of a feeling for fashion, it was just simple poverty.

TAYLOR: Of course when we get – may I?

MUGGERIDGE: Oh do, take anything off you like – do you want me to take my trousers off?

TAYLOR: No – no – no, not at the moment. I would say the trousers, incidentally, are rather baggy and they look a – your braces haven't broken, have they, Mr Muggeridge?

MUGGERIDGE: No, I don't think so. The whole thing is holding up, I'm glad to say.

TAYLOR: They could do without the turn-up, I think. But again, getting back to this grey thing – grey – grey – grey – grey – grey – and suddenly brown boots and blue socks.

MUGGERIDGE: Not boots, old boy, shoes.

TAYLOR: And blue socks – don't you think this is –

MUGGERIDGE: Is it a little indelicate?

TAYLOR: I think so – yes.

MUGGERIDGE: Of course I'm no expert on this matter, but I would awfully like to look at your very elegant get up. Now this particular double-breasted waistcoat – is that a fashionable thing?

TAYLOR: Well that helps with the new fashion, the padded stomach –

MUGGERIDGE: Now this tie of yours –

TAYLOR: – you don't like that?

MUGGERIDGE: Well, I wouldn't say I don't like it, I just think it's a tiny bit fanciful.

TAYLOR: Well, of course I'm a fanciful person.

MUGGERIDGE: And what about this little flower here?

TAYLOR: Well that is a compliment to you, Mr Muggeridge – I must say that I'm rather surprised you didn't return this compliment.

MUGGERIDGE: And what about these trousers of yours – they seem to be a bit spidery, you know.

TAYLOR: Spidery?

MUGGERIDGE: Mmm.

TAYLOR: Well no – you see, there's a fine strong leg within it to sustain –

MUGGERIDGE: I'm sure of that – yes.

TAYLOR: – that's probably why you have to build yours out a little wider –

MUGGERIDGE: You mean to cover these old lean shanks?

TAYLOR: That could be it –

MUGGERIDGE: And what about these shoes? – I think they're rather like slippers.

TAYLOR: Slippers?

MUGGERIDGE: You couldn't walk out in those shoes, could you?

TAYLOR: I can keep them on – yes –

MUGGERIDGE: And hold them on?

TAYLOR: I still have my arches, of course.

MUGGERIDGE: You have your arches. Now do you, as a matter of fact, keep your socks up with a suspender or by will power?

TAYLOR: Well I actually hook them over my leg muscle – that would be another problem for you, wouldn't it?

MUGGERIDGE: Could we just take a peep at the lower leg – there's nothing indelicate –

TAYLOR: Yes indeed –

MUGGERIDGE: Very good indeed. But isn't that a tiny bit chilly?

TAYLOR: No – no – no – I'm a warm-blooded person.

MUGGERIDGE: Mr Taylor, long combinations do not –

TAYLOR: Oh, never at all –

MUGGERIDGE: – play any role in your life at all?

TAYLOR: You don't wear them at all, do you, Mr Muggeridge?

MUGGERIDGE: Well I prefer not to go into that, but I was just asking you, that you don't in fact do anything of that sort?

TAYLOR: No, nothing of that sort.

MUGGERIDGE: Mr Taylor, do you regard fashion for men as a very edifying thing?

TAYLOR: Oh I certainly do. I mean, what do you expect me to say? Of course I do, my whole life depends upon it.

Secretaries

I've suffered a great deal from secretaries in my life; I'm practically a sort of martyr to secretaries. If there was a special kind of disease, like housemaid's knee, if you could have secretary's thumb, I would have it.

The English Cardinal

A personal view of
John Carmel Heenan, Archbishop of Westminster

In back numbers of *Punch* funny bishops and curates abound. Similarly in novels of clerical life, like Trollope's *Barchester Towers*. But there are no funny Cardinals. The traditional English scene just doesn't seem to accommodate them. Yet Cardinals indubitably exist. Witness John Carmel Heenan, our only extant specimen; Archbishop of Westminster, and head of the Roman Catholic Church in England; the English Cardinal.

MUGGERIDGE: I always feel that almost the only reason that I'd like to become a Cardinal would be to be waited on by nuns.

CARDINAL: I think you'd make a very good Cardinal as a matter of fact.

MUGGERIDGE: I doubt it strongly. Not a Cardinal, perhaps a bishop.

CARDINAL: Well, you've got to start somewhere.

MUGGERIDGE: I always like lunching on Fridays because we don't have meat.

CARDINAL: You're not getting any fish, by the way, you're getting an omelette.

MUGGERIDGE: No, no, it's very nice. This would be part of the Catholic life that I would find least difficult. I suppose it dates from a time when eating meat was a tremendously important thing.

CARDINAL: Well, you know what they say. They say that it was an example of the Jewish instinct of the twelve Apostles; they were all fishermen, and they decided that if they made a rule about fish on Fridays, it would be good business. But I don't think that's theological doctrine.

MUGGERIDGE: How powerful is a Cardinal today?

CARDINAL: How powerful? It really depends on what you mean by power.

MUGGERIDGE: But aren't you the boss of the bishops?

CARDINAL: The boss of the bishops? No, the Pope is.

MUGGERIDGE: But he's your boss?

CARDINAL: The Pope is my boss, but he's also the boss of all the bishops. The Pope deals directly with the bishops, not through me necessarily.

MUGGERIDGE: He can go over your head as it were?

CARDINAL: Well, yes. I wouldn't think of it in that way.

MUGGERIDGE: No. But the thing is that of course the Church does indulge in the sort of magnificence and outward show which one associates with worldly power.

CARDINAL: When you're taking part in ritual, as I do very often, it is burdensome rather than self-glorifying.

MUGGERIDGE: You mean you personally don't like it too much?

CARDINAL: Well, no, and also you've got to wear the robes. The same as the poor Queen when she wears the crown and the royal robes. I'm sure she's most uncomfortable but nevertheless she knows that by doing this she gives a certain satisfaction to her people.

MUGGERIDGE: To me, at any rate, such emulation of the trappings of earthly authority would seem to have a certain danger.

CARDINAL: This outward panoply and foolishness that you are thinking of, this has its uses, because even sticking a chain round a man's neck and calling him mayor of Wigan – I don't mean that with any disrespect to Wigan, of course – but putting a chain round a man's neck marks him out as chief citizen. If he's not a fool he doesn't really think he's the brightest and best and most intelligent man in that particular town. Nevertheless, that chain of office shows him to be what he is; it's a sign – a badge of his office. Incidentally, I've got a chain on too, with a Cross, and I always envy a Mayor his chain, because at the end of the year he can just take it off and go off on his own, but this thing will be with me until I'm in the coffin in the Cathedral. . . .

Cardinal Heenan's own origin and background – Irish extraction, lower middle class – have been no impediment to his elevation to his present eminence. Indeed, these antecedents become the Roman Catholic Church in England better than, say, a seat in the House of Lords. A large proportion of the English Roman Catholic Church's four million or so members are Irish,

or of Irish extraction. There is a small admixture of aristocrats from the old English Catholic families and a few notable intellectual camp followers. But in the main English Roman Catholics tend to be artisans and poor. This may partly account for the continuing appeal of a glittering liturgy and ceremonial: the poor need dreams of magnificence to compensate for the bareness of their lives. Only Quakers are rich enough to worship austerely.

MUGGERIDGE: How about your role as proselytizer?

CARDINAL: I loathe that word.

MUGGERIDGE: Presumably you want more people to become Roman Catholics?

CARDINAL: Yes. I want everybody to.

MUGGERIDGE: Therefore you are a sort of missionary.

CARDINAL: I object to the word proselytizer because it sounds like something very underhand, some poison, some snaky movement by which you're trying to drag people from the truth and indoctrinate them.... No, you wouldn't call Christ a proselytizer; a preacher perhaps. We call the Apostles –

MUGGERIDGE: Evangelists.

CARDINAL: Evangelists, men who have the message, which they

believe to be true, and want to spread it everywhere. Now there's nothing strange about that, because even if you happened to have discovered a cough cure and it really works, and you take this thing, this drug or injection, all winter, and never have a cold, you know well that you cannot stop telling your friends about it. If you're a good man and you possess a good thing, you want to share it. There's an old philosophical saying, *Bonum est diffusivum sui*. You'll know this, of course, but for the sake of my colleagues on the bench I will translate. It means that goodness diffuses itself, spreads itself, it can't help it, just as heat can't help expanding, warmth glows. In this kind of way a person who possesses the faith wants to spread it, wants his warmth to go out to others. Now that's no problem to me. Is it a problem to you?

MUGGERIDGE: No, not a problem at all.

CARDINAL: But this is what you've got to remember. Although we don't use the word because it's an offensive kind of word to use, this country's full of pagans, this country's full of people who know as little about God as the so-called heathens that you mentioned.

MUGGERIDGE: Since you would hold that your Church in certain respects has the message uniquely, you would presumably wish good Anglicans also to join it.

CARDINAL: Well naturally; after all this country was once a completely Catholic country, as you know. It would be lovely if once again it could be a completely Catholic country, from my point of view. Whereas, as you know, others would say, 'Oh no, just a moment, it was once a Catholic country, but then the corruption of Rome spread, and it had to be cured by a complete revival and renewal, and then the old Catholic faith was restored and Romanism dissipated.' That's another point of view – not, as it happens, mine.

MUGGERIDGE: I didn't think it was. Anyway, the point is that presumably, in so far as you would in the long run hope to bring back the Anglican church into the fold, into the Roman Catholic fold, that would mean that you were a missionary in relation to them also; that even the Archbishop of Canterbury, say, is a target.

CARDINAL: Well, target is hardly the word.

MUGGERIDGE: How do you get along with him, incidentally?

CARDINAL: He's a very great friend of mine; I'm very fond of him, and of his wife too.

MUGGERIDGE: Do you argue with him when you're there?

CARDINAL: I don't think we argue in the sense of having controversy. It's clear that as the Chief Bishop of the Church, the Anglican Church in this country and throughout the world, it's hardly likely that when I go to Lambeth I would go with a whole bundle of tracts in my pocket and say, 'Look, I must explain to you about Papal infallibility.' Of course not. Our conversation is on a very different kind of level, and I don't think he ever seriously tries to persuade me of the errors of Rome or offer me a job as his assistant or auxiliary bishop in Canterbury. No, we don't do that. But if you ask me, I don't want to appear in any way insincere. I do agree that my greatest desire would be to have all Englishmen Catholics again.

MUGGERIDGE: And those little churches and cathedrals that used to be Catholic – all their bells would be ringing.

In Rome, of course, bells of Catholic churches have been ringing longer and more loudly than anywhere else. In Rome, the centre of Christianity since its beginning some 2,000 years ago, Cardinal Heenan's position is both magnified and reduced – magnified because he is part of a universal church rather than head of a minority communion – reduced because he is one Cardinal among many instead of the unique specimen. There are many Cardinals but only one Pope.

The Ecumenical Council, somewhat impulsively called by Pope Paul's predecessor, Pope John, has been inescapably confronted with some of the most explosive dilemmas of our time. The twentieth century, it would seem, has broken into one of the last and most powerful citadels holding out against its incursions. Yet, in the eyes of an outsider like myself, this seems more of a lavishly mounted spectacular than a solemn act of worship.

These Cardinals and Bishops – such extraordinary and diverse old faces! Such a variety of races and nationalities! These are the appointed custodians of the rock on which, in their estimation, the whole structure of Christendom has been founded. None more so than Cardinal Heenan. He has been educated, brought up, trained for that very purpose. He

looks round on a world full of doubt and uncertainty and re-
joices the more in his own certainties. Then the scene changes,
the authority that's everything seems to be wavering. The rock
itself is shaken. Basic concepts like original sin lose their fine
definition. Is it possible that concupiscence, fortified by the
birth pill, is after all permissible? Can it be Lady Chatterley
approaching the altar rails?

Rome is for Cardinal Heenan almost as much home territory
as London or Liverpool. He was a student at the English College and the Georgian University here. Yet I should not say
myself that he seems more at home than he does in St James's
Park. All unusual men, I have noticed, give an impression of
being strangers in a strange land; only mediocrities easily
acclimatize themselves to their mortality. Yet it is, of course,
impossible really to get inside someone else's skin, least of all a
demolition man inside a custodian's. Yet one can, without
presumption, sense in Cardinal Heenan the strain and even the
anguish of seeing cherished beliefs under attack. Not just from
without – that's taken for granted, that's what martyrdom,
which he has been taught to believe is a Christian's highest destiny, is about – but from within the Church itself.

CARDINAL: You've got to be quite mature before you realize
what being a priest involves, particularly in the question of
celibacy, giving up the right to a family and so on, and it's at
that time, I think, that the crisis comes with most people. These
young men realize, they might be 20, 19, 21, anything, but
they'll be quite mature and they will then say, 'Now, for the
first time I realize that this really does mean a lonely life.'
You're not feeling miserable because you're alone, but you're a
man apart.

The relationship between a Catholic priest and his people is
something you've got to experience to understand, they call me
Father and that's a term of tremendous affection. Now that
Fatherhood I find enormously attractive and uplifting, but the
shouting and the kissing, that means very little indeed.

MUGGERIDGE: What do people want from their religion?

CARDINAL: It's the unchanging teaching of the Church which
answers the deepest appeal, I think, in the heart of the people.

MUGGERIDGE: What is that unchanging teaching, in a word?

CARDINAL: In a word, if you want *a* word – authority.

MUGGERIDGE: Authority, whose authority?

CARDINAL: The authority of the Church, made known through the Pope and through the Council.

MUGGERIDGE: Contrasting with that, when you're standing at the altar . . .?

CARDINAL: Now that's quite different. When I'm standing at the altar, I am there representing Christ. When I offer the Mass, I don't say, 'This is the Body of Christ,' I say, 'This is my Body,' because I, John Heenan, don't exist. That's why the vestments are there to disguise my personality. I am standing there as a mediator, as one representing Christ. That's quite different; there I am the Church, so to speak.

MUGGERIDGE: This is the difficult thing to understand.

CARDINAL: Of course, of course.

MUGGERIDGE: I mean, how do you feel, when you're doing it?

CARDINAL: Well, I've been a priest for thirty-five years, and I've offered Mass every day.

MUGGERIDGE: For thirty-five years.

CARDINAL: Yes, and sometimes more than once a day. Now, there's an old saying, an old Latin saw, – *Ab assuetis non fit passio* – a thing you're used to doesn't affect you, and so, obviously, I don't feel emotionally now as I did the day I put on vestments for the first time, and offered my first Mass as a young priest. I don't feel the same but perhaps I treasure the Mass even more; the Mass means more to me now after thirty-five years of celebration daily, than it did then. But how to describe that and how to show that that should be so is very difficult.

MUGGERIDGE: Does it add to your worries when you think that by and large people are falling away from the Christian religion?

CARDINAL: Of course, of course. I don't use the word worry, because I don't worry about these things. It's God's business, you know. If they're falling away from religion, they're falling away from Him.

MUGGERIDGE: But you wouldn't feel that it's because you're being inadequate?

CARDINAL: Yes, yes.

MUGGERIDGE: Do you, when you wake up in the night, think that . . .

CARDINAL: How do you know I wake up in the night?

MUGGERIDGE: I'm sure you're a fellow-insomniac. I can spot them. When you wake up, would it be a thing that would worry you to think to yourself, 'Well, are we really making a great mistake'?

CARDINAL: No, I don't. On this, no. I have no doubts whatever.

MUGGERIDGE: You would regard yourself as being a person who held, on the whole, for tradition?

CARDINAL: Well yes, I would say that every Catholic really at heart values the tradition. You can't be a Catholic without holding for tradition. We're the one thing in a changing world that's solid. We're the thing that people can reach for.

MUGGERIDGE: But you are going to go on being as solid as you have been?

CARDINAL: I hope so. Of course we are. Rome is the centre of Christianity. This place is still the centre, and that's not because of that material building. Because, you see, this city of Rome could be taken over by the communists tomorrow, or next year. But even if materially we abandoned Rome, the spiritual centre of the Church is the Pope, the Vicar of Christ, and, as you know, there have been Popes that have never seen Rome. At one time there were no less than three people claiming to be the Pope. There was vice in this Vatican. This was a centre of vice from time to time, the Borgia Popes and so on, and therefore we are sometimes inclined to think that this was the most wicked of all ages, but in fact, in many ways, it's the best of all ages. And you asked some time ago where I stood, and was I against progress. The answer is no. But obviously when you get people emotionally charged and determined to broaden the view, there are going to be excesses, they're going to exaggerate, they're going to get it wrong, and some of us have got to stand quite firm and say, 'Yes, I love this wide open view, but we mustn't for a moment forget truth, we mustn't pretend that truth doesn't matter.'

I put to myself these questions about Cardinal Heenan: A hard man? I shouldn't say so; severe, perhaps, though even that more in outward appearance than inward temperament. Severe certainly with himself. An ambitious man? Yes, but only in the sense of wanting to fulfil to the uttermost his priestly functions. An intolerant man? Undoubtedly with, for instance, the uncertainties and hesitancies of intellectuals. A narrow man? In a way, yes. An evangelist through and through, wrapped up in pastoral duties and responsibilities, wholly concerned with propagating the Faith, of which he has a clear, but possibly oversimplified version. A good man? Who can tell? Lacking some elements of greatness, like a wide vision and the imaginative gifts to project it, but possessing others, like clarity, sincerity and an all-absorbing passion to carry out God's will; underneath the surface confidence, a touching and true humility which I have glimpsed from time to time. A great and formidable priest, anyway, for the mid-twentieth century.

Royal Command Performance

I would choose simply what I thought was the best film, and I confess I wouldn't mind very much whether the Royal Family enjoyed it or not.

The Establishment

Every time I see the Archbishop of Canterbury on the screen I am conscious that – to adapt a famous saying of Voltaire – if he did not exist it would be impossible to invent him. Efforts to ridicule those set in authority over us are constantly frustrated by their own intrinsic ridiculousness. I mean, who can hope to improve on the original of, say, a George Brown or a Ted Heath? Their native absurdity exceeds by far the wildest and most fantastic inventions. These public figures are snatching the bread out of the mouths of professional entertainers just by being themselves. Why shouldn't they have to join Equity and submit their scripts to the Lord Chamberlain like everyone else? Why, for that matter, shouldn't they come on *The Late Show* and save John Bird the trouble of impersonating them? Here an awesome thought strikes me. Perhaps they do.

The Established Church

The identification of a church and a state is about as farcical as a vegetarian joining the Butcher's Union.

The Ten Commandments

My own view of the Ten Commandments is very like that of an Anglican Bishop who once said, and I think it's very typical of the whole Anglican Church, that they are like an examination paper – eight only to be attempted.

Is an Elite Necessary?

A discussion with
Lord James of Rusholme and Bertrand Russell

MUGGERIDGE: I'm terribly sceptical about this whole business of an élite. Of course I think in any sort of society, whatever its nature, you get people who have an enormous desire for power and they will grab power – they'll find some means of getting it. If it's the money society, they'll get a lot of money, and if it's a Communist society, they'll become members of the Communist Party and get power. The thing in them is the desire for power. But I'm terribly sceptical about this idea that you can sit down and say, 'We want an élite, that is how we're going to produce it.'

JAMES: It isn't only political power. It is really in some ways the setting of values and standards for the rest of society. I disagree, I think, probably with Muggeridge over this. He had shown the whole weakness of the people who say 'We don't want an élite' by admitting that some people will grab power. I think the fundamental point about a democracy is that it must organize itself in such a way that the right people – the people who deserve it, who will exercise it rightly – have the positions of authority.

MUGGERIDGE: Well I think that's crying for the moon.

RUSSELL: I think the desire for power is by no means evidence that a man ought to have power. Quite clearly Hitler had an enormous desire for power and it didn't do any good that he should have it. What you want is some way of sifting out people according to their capacity to do a job, but I don't think that it ought to apply to the politician. I think that politics in a narrower sense ought to be still the place where the plain man's opinions count. I think it's the executive jobs where you want the élite.

JAMES: I entirely agree, because in the classical idea of the élite, I mean Plato's *Republic*, there his guardians specifically don't want power, it's one of their characteristics of course, rightly or wrongly.

MUGGERIDGE: Well I don't want to be purely obstructionist but I think that in any circumstances it would be terribly easy to define, as Plato did, the sort of people you want as your élite, and I know exactly that I would like to be governed always by humane, kindly, delightful, intelligent people, but I think that when you've said that, you've said absolutely nothing. In fact that isn't how the world works, and I myself am terribly sceptical about this idea that you sit down and say, 'Now if we can produce people who have passed this exam, or people who have passed this intelligence test, or people who are born into this particular class, that is our élite.'

RUSSELL: I agree with you as against Plato's guardians because I think Plato was quite unrealistic in supposing that the guardians would not grab power. I think they would have grabbed power and presently, as one has seen in Russia, they will also grab money. I said in 1920 that Russia was exactly Plato's republic and it shocked the Platonists and shocked the Russians, but I still think it was true.

MUGGERIDGE: And enormously to your credit you said it in my humble opinion.

RUSSELL: When I was in Russia in 1920 they complained that the only people they could get to do the work of bank clerks were ordinary seamen because everybody else was against the banks and of course the ordinary seamen didn't do the sums right.

JAMES: What it your alternative, Muggeridge, to this idea? I mean are you just going to leave those setting of standards for the whole society, the possession of this executive power, that Russell was talking about, are you going to leave that just to the naked operation of the market?

MUGGERIDGE: In a sense yes. I myself take the view that power is an abhorrent thing, and it's a most unfortunate circumstance of life that it's necessary to have people to exert power. I'd much prefer to live in a world in which that wasn't so, but since I have to recognize that it is so, I am inclined to think that what you've got to do is to let those people who want it and want it desperately get it, and I think that all your arrangements, which of course nowadays are very popular, for training people and picking them out and having intelligence tests and character tests, ultimately will prove a complete failure.

JAMES: But I'm sure that your whole idea of power is much too narrow a one. You're thinking of it entirely in terms of political power.

MUGGERIDGE: I'm not.

JAMES: In the modern set-up what you've got to think of is the administrator – professional administrator – who's not obviously a sort of man who loves power or enjoys the exercise of it. You've got further the scientist and the technologist. You've got further the person who in the aesthetic and general culture field sets the standard for a great ignorant democracy. Now those people are exercising great power.

MUGGERIDGE: I quite agree.

JAMES: But they don't call it power.

MUGGERIDGE: I don't think you can choose them.

RUSSELL: Take a perfectly concrete thing. Take agriculture. The amount of agricultural land in England is small in proportion to the population and it's very desirable that the agricultural land should be profitably farmed. Now, the immense majority of farmers have an absolute contempt for scientific agriculture and unless you compel or induce them they will ignore everything that is known about how land should be farmed and that ought not to be allowed.

MUGGERIDGE: Try as you will to arrive at those people who can most usefully cultivate the very limited land in this country, in fact the people who will most usefully cultivate it will be the people who want to cultivate it primarily for reasons, alas, of cupidity.

JAMES: Well I'm sorry but that isn't really true today any longer. You see, if you take Russell's example, which is a very good one, of agriculture, there is a new class of technologists who are not going to make anything more than a salary out of it. They represent the new élite as it were.

MUGGERIDGE: Well, I believe in the naked operation of human passion.

JAMES: You have a democratic educational system in which you attempt as far as possible to give some sort of opportunity to every person whatever their background; and you choose those people who are more intelligent than other people, and you give them a different sort of education.

MUGGERIDGE: Well I would only say this, that if the affairs of our country were flourishing at this moment, our foreign service was distinguishing itself in every part of the world, then I think James's proposition would stand up very well, but what I discover as a journalist wandering about this world is that these people in fact know absolutely nothing about what they're supposed to be doing. They were all chosen, they've all got through this mesh, they've all distinguished themselves in this terrific process for choosing an élite. My goodness how badly they're doing – how badly they're doing.

JAMES: Good gracious, what an extraordinary picture of the world you have if I may say so. How long do you think we've had real secondary education in this country? Fifty-four years, and you see it hasn't grown up in that time.

MUGGERIDGE: The thing is that this system of choosing an élite by means of intellectual tests has operated now for quite a time and in my opinion it has been a total failure.

RUSSELL: It seems to me that our Civil Service is imperfect because we still attach too much importance to a classical education and not enough to science.

MUGGERIDGE: Yes, but the methods that we're adopting, and I'm sure they're most honourably conceived, are in fact methods which do not catch the right people.

JAMES: Oh I see. It's the methods now, not the principle.

MUGGERIDGE: Yes, of course it's the methods. You set up certain examinations, certain tests, and you say, I will apply those tests and I will produce splendid, brilliant, effective administrators; and I say to you that those particular people that you choose have in actual practice not done very well, and it occurs to me that because they haven't done very well, this whole idea of choosing people in that way may not be the right system.

JAMES: I want to know what's wrong with the methods.

MUGGERIDGE: What's wrong with the methods is that you are basing your test primarily on intelligence.

RUSSELL: All men have equal rights in certain respects, but that doesn't mean that they are equal. I mean, nobody would maintain that everybody is fit to be Prime Minister.

MUGGERIDGE: I would use the simple method that the man who wishes to exert power gets power.

JAMES: But that gives us Hitler.

MUGGERIDGE: Yes. It gives us Napoleon, it gives us Lenin, it gives us Roosevelt, it gives us all the people who've exercised power in our time. But I hate them all because I hate power.

JAMES: You must admit that they're all pretty intelligent.

MUGGERIDGE: Yes, but they'd have failed in the Manchester Grammar School.

JAMES: Have you any conceivable evidence for that whatever? Have you any idea what the Manchester Grammar School exam is like?

RUSSELL: We know that Napoleon was quite a good mathematician.

MUGGERIDGE: Where I think that this whole business of an élite goes wrong is that it's a dream. It's the same dream as the platonic dream.

RUSSELL: It isn't a dream. If you take the ordinary person whose IQ is, we'll say, 90 and compare him with a person whose IQ is 120, nobody can deny that there is a difference which is quite obvious; and if you put the man whose IQ is 90 in a position of power, he will infallibly make a mess of it. The first man may, but he certainly will.

MUGGERIDGE: But is it really true, Lord Russell, that the man with the high IQ is good at his job? The only man of action I've ever cared for is Lincoln who was a very attractive person; and I always remember that wonderful story about him and Grant, who was a drunkard. People said, 'This is a terrible thing, you've got a General who's a drunkard,' and Lincoln said, 'Grant wins battles and I wish all my Generals were drunkards.' This seems to me the essence of the thing, that if you've got Generals you want them to win battles, and you don't care whether they're frightfully good at the staff college.

JAMES: What has that got to do with it? What we're saying is that on the whole Generals will win battles when they're more intelligent. I mean the number of battles that have been lost by a jolly good, pure ivory-headed chap must be absolutely legion. Your argument really rests on misconception about this idea of intelligence. Would you be interested to know that in the last war 95 per cent of the subalterns were drawn from the top five per cent of the population as regards intelligence. But you wouldn't really think that subalterns were intellectuals, would you?

MUGGERIDGE: Speaking of my own small experience of the war, I really can't mention names here, but of two Generals one was a complete failure and was intellectually very distinguished, and the other was fantastically successful and was, from a purely intellectual point of view, one of the most foolish men I've ever met.

JAMES: By your standards.

MUGGERIDGE: By any standards.

JAMES: He was probably in the top five per cent of the population.

MUGGERIDGE: Oh not at all.

JAMES: He would certainly have been to the staff college.

MUGGERIDGE: Minor point, minor point. But the fact is, you see, I think these particular tests that you apply do not measure people who are capable of doing this mysterious and abhorrent thing of governing and controlling their fellows.

JAMES: What I am saying is that high intelligence is not a sufficient criterion; it is a necessary prerequisite.

Facts

If I was a praying man, which unfortunately I'm not, I should pray to be delivered from facts, and I'm sure that when our civilization finally sinks, and the waves close over its head, it will be because it's stuffed, stupefied with facts.

Our Own Correspondent

Newsgathering in Washington

In 1946 just after I had been demobilized I reached the conclusion that Washington had become the centre of the world. I felt just the same in 1932 about Moscow and went there as Correspondent for the *Manchester Guardian*. Now I wanted to go to Washington which I duly managed to do. This time as Correspondent for the *Daily Telegraph*. I stayed there for two years. It really was the centre of the world I found, but oh God, what a world. I reached the conclusion that I'd rather be on the periphery and left with relief.

Then last year I went back – the first time for twenty years – to have another look around. The same old honeypot of news, the same swarm of newsgatherers buzzing around it. I, thank God, have got no more buzz left in me. But in Washington I found the buzzing is louder than ever.

For me as a newsgatherer the day began with the newspapers. On a Sunday morning, I'd pick – or rather gather – them up on my way to my office in the National Press Building. What a load! Like a Grubb Street Messiah bearing on my back all the world's woes and troubles – in newsprint, of course. The truth is that news, like beauty, is in the eye of the beholder. If all the newsgatherers, all the rotary presses and all the teleprinters and all the television cameras were silenced, shut up, there would be no news.

News in the newsgatherers' sense bears the same relation to events as muzak does to music. Journalism is tremendously a matters of taking in each other's washing. We can generally find something in one of the newspapers. Coming from London to be sent back there. It's like a wonderful game of transatlantic tennis, you know. James Reston is in Washington. Then pick out what James Reston says, hit it back to London. State Department sources, informed circles back here, catch it in the net and bang it down again. Off to London again. Fifteen all.

In each news office the same scene is enacted – the same ticker-tapes churning out the same words, but scrutinized by different eyes looking for different treasure. A news broiler house – kept at an even temperature, identical lighting and food for all, but each of us expected to lay his own personalized eggs, in the shape of exclusive stories, fashioned and angled for our particular readers. Our Own Correspondent's very own eggs . . . unfertilized, of course.

Where there's power, there's news. And of course vice versa. Journalists follow power as sharks follow a ship, hoping that it will either sink or someone will fall off. So when I came to Washington my steps instinctively led me to the White House, 1600 Pennsylvania Avenue. A residence, not a palace. The house of the top common man.

GUARD: Yes, sir, may I help you?

MUGGERIDGE: Well, I'm a British journalist actually and I'm looking for news. Somehow I thought there might be some news in here.

GUARD: Well, sir, did you have an appointment or do you have a pass or something?

MUGGERIDGE: Well, I've got my passport.

GUARD: OK, fine. Will you step into the office, please?

Inside the White House there are always some journalists keeping vigil. Day and night – they also serve who only sit and sleep. After all, you never know. Suddenly the word can come – he's shot, he's dead; he's out, he's in – shaking them out of their lethargy like athletes for telephones, microphones; pounding frenziedly at their typewriters.

Who governs America? It was a question I often put to myself in my newsgathering days here, without ever finding a wholly satisfying answer. In the Cabinet Room, at any rate, what passes for being the Government meets and deliberates. Here, in my day, sat Harry Truman, still not quite used to the authority which had so unexpectedly fallen on him, as he put it, out of the sky. Little men – shall we? shan't we? shall we what? – blow the earth and all mankind to smithereens? It's almost funny. Perhaps, after all, that's how the world does end – with little men seated at a table.

HOWARD K. SMITH: Thomas Jefferson, the most brilliant President, had a bad habit of staring and wouldn't have been good on television. And Abraham Lincoln wouldn't have gone over too well because frankly he had ugly features that wouldn't show up very well.

MUGGERIDGE: And very eccentric ways?

SMITH: Yes, and a bad twang, a little like the man from Texas who's there now. We finally decided the only two men who could really have done extremely well would be Warren Harding and Franklin Pierce who had been listed as the two worst presidents we ever had.

The president is now a pope and emperor combined. As newsgatherers we had to keep an eye on his court and its doings. What, I used to ask myself, would the Founding Fathers have thought of their Chief Executive, so carefully hedged round with checks and balances, blossoming out into twentieth-century Charlemagne presiding over an Unholy American Empire on which the sun never rises?

The State Department, after the White House, was our most frequent port of call. In my day, in the old Executive Building adjoining the White House; now in its own Byzantine quarters – erected on what used to be a marsh known as Foggy Bottom. A weird blend of the Old and the New Worlds; like one of those marriages American heiresses used to make with European princelings. It might almost be Monaco – the gimcrack elegance, the period pieces languishing outside all periods. An anteroom leads to the sacred precincts where the Secretary of State himself reads dispatches, receives visiting nobilities, and struggles with the impossible task of devising an American foreign policy that sounds like the Declaration of Independence. We newsgatherers had to try and extract nourishment in the shape of news out of those marble halls.

IZZIE STONE: Every government agency now has its own little brigade or even regiment of press officers who are anxious to help your quotation marks by giving you press releases and pre-fabricated copy and mis-answering your questions and deluding you. They'll tell you a lot of things 'off the record' that aren't true and hope that you'll print it on your own responsibility, as something coming from a high source, or an informed source or a source close to the White House. I always think of people who have sources quite close to the White House ... I know the peanut vendor on the corner.

MUGGERIDGE: He's very close.

In the beginning was the NEWS, and the NEWS became words. Words printed, words sent through space on waves of light and sound. Words spoken, words written. Oceans of ink, acres upon acres of newsprint, miles of tape and film – all bearing *news*. Bombarding the senses, stupefying the mind; unceasing, night and day, winter and summer. Catastrophies, hopes and joys; sorrows and inanities, the weather, wars and rumours of wars. News-breakers endlessly beating against the shores of time. Into this maelstrom we emptied our little buckets, our offerings soon swept away and lost to view. Everything recorded, everything explored, everything expounded, to become – nothing.

In Washington I was my own legman – not so easy in America where pedestrians are suspect and traffic rules all. I used to think of my places of call as Stations of the Cross, pausing at each – White House, State, Commerce, Treasury, Interior – to beat my breast. *Mea Culpa*, give us this day our daily story; then on to the next.

Up Massachusetts Avenue where all the Embassies are – a long haul to the British Embassy. Embassies also yield stories and have public relations radar screens to ensure that one lands at one's allotted berth. 'Anything cooking, old boy?' From one old boy to another old boy with sometimes, as a special treat, admission to a *real* diplomat who knew *real* secrets. In my time this usually turned out to be Donald Maclean.

On Capitol Hill there sits the august Congress of the United States. The Senate and the House of Representatives and all their associate officials. Here assemble the elected tribunes of the people to deliberate and discuss, to advise and consent. Here, it might be supposed, if anywhere, news must proliferate. After all, these Senators and Congressman are lords of creation, at least in their own estimation. My memories of them are of floods of old-style rhetoric rarely deviating into sense; of ungainly men with spittoons beside them who paw one another and doggedly obstruct all legislative proposals; of interminable committee hearings and investigations pursued, of statements of the obvious, obviously stated.

(*Speaking immersed to neck in turkish bath*) I always think of Washington as a sort of turkish bath. This isn't just because it's hot and steamy and soporific often. Once I was working here and in need of reparation, I had a turkish bath. It was in an establishment long since defunct, called if I remember correctly, rather unappetizingly, Ringworm Hall. The apparatus was extremely antique, and indeed seemed almost to be falling to pieces. None the less, the place had a considerable social cache, and when I came to and began to peer through the steam I saw quite near me the familiar features of none other than the then British Ambassador, Lord Inverchapel, a curious figure, a man with a rather large nose and naturally very rubicund. Of course in those circumstances, more so than ever. And I'd just been warned off the British Embassy for being what is called 'unhelpful'. I thought it best to avert my eyes, exchanging a wink, however, with his private secretary who was being steamed beside him, presumably to be on hand if some prescient thought or remark was steamed out of his Excellency.

Somehow the scene has stayed with me. It seems very symbolic somehow of this Federal capital whose only industry is government and whose only output is words, words ceaselessly produced like steam, and then distilled into heavy drops of information, which in turn evaporated again into steam.

ART BUCHWALD: Newspapers particularly are in the manufacturing business and you have to manufacture news or you don't sell newspapers. Now television is different. They have either to get the cameras where there is news or when they get there they make the news by the fact that they're there.

HOWARD K. SMITH: A good example is this young Negro, Stokeley Carmichael, a natural-born, 100 per cent, 26-carat failure. He went down to Alabama and tried to enlist the rural Negroes and they wouldn't listen to him. He went to cities, he came here to Washington, he went to Roosevelt High School – the all-Negro High School – tried to arouse them. Twelve Negroes came to hear him speak and they booed him. But then once he was walking in Mississippi and saw lots of reporters and cameramen following James Meredith, so he ran and shouted, 'Burn the honkey, let's have black power,' and all the cameras and all the reporters raced after him and they followed him for ever after.

MUGGERIDGE: He was made.

SMITH: Yes. Whitney Young, the genuine Negro leader in this country, said the other day that Stokeley Carmichael has a following of fifty Negroes and about five thousand white reporters.

BUCHWALD: All of our better riots are really caused by television. Everybody's sitting around minding their own business, sitting on the steps and suddenly the TV cameras arrive and pow you have a riot, and then they have some film to show. Well, what scares you about this is that it could be a hundred people having a demonstration, but when you see it on TV it looks like the whole country has gone berserk.

Abraham Lincoln, in his memorial, looks down on the Federal Capital he so valiantly preserved for posterity. What does he make of it now – so vast a concentration of wealth and power with, behind it, so infirm a purpose? I too, as a newsgatherer, a little satellite riding through its stratosphere, look down, trying to find the mainspring, the driving force. Not in the stale rhetoric hanging like a cloud over Capitol Hill, surely. Nor in the White House's tired, dispirited tenant. Not in the Treasury's paper treasure. Nor in the Pentagon generals waiting for orders. No guiding light in the briefings and handouts so plentifully provided. Where then? Or has your Union, dear Abe, turned into a fantasy; an American Dream indeed, from which we shall all – perhaps soon – have to awaken?

Television

Just imagine! At this very moment all over the world – by muddy banks of tropical rivers, in remote deserts and tangled jungle and frozen Arctic wastes – people are watching *Peyton Place*. Or, if that hasn't reached them yet, some old print of *I Love Lucy* or *Wagon Train*. Isn't it terrific! Various attempts have been made to unify mankind – the Holy Roman Empire, the Comintern, the United Nations. Where they all failed *Batman* has succeeded; he, not the *Internationale* (as we sang in the old revolutionary hymn), unites the human race.

This universality of the telly has been all too little noticed in the celebrations of its various anniversaries. A Pope may claim to say mass for scores or even hundreds of millions of Catholics, Communist leaders in their more ebullient moments when they gather on Lenin's tomb are liable to speak of the toiling masses everywhere who look to them for guidance, but how can they compete with *The Man from UNCLE*, welcome at every hearth and home on earth, and, I dare say, in due course in the universe beyond. I feel sure that the first American astronauts to land on the moon will pipe in *UNCLE* long before they get round to Jesus Christ, or even L.B.J.

There's another thing: through this universal telly the so-called backward or under-developed nations of the world can see in advance the glorious possibilities which lie before them when they become advanced and civilized. It should prove a tremendous incentive to effort and endurance – all those wonderful pills and potions they're going to be able to swallow to cure all the wonderful ailments which are going to afflict them; all the wonderful wars and liberations, all the wonderful pile-ups on all the wonderful highways, all the wonderful marriages and divorces and race-riots which lie before them. Why, they must be saying to themselves, if we work hard at our studies and pay due attention to what the Peace Corps man tells us, we'll be able to *read Peyton Place* as well as see it on the telly. If that thought doesn't get them moving along the road to progress and prosperity, then nothing will.

This is the first time in human history that, thanks to television, the uncivilized have been presented with a visual preview of what civilization holds in store for them. One likes to think that, had the Goths and Vandals been able to envisage Governor

Reagan, H. Wilson, the Beatles and other choice twentieth-century items, they would have tiptoed back to their forest fastnesses and stayed there instead of advancing on Rome. I fear, however, that no such caution will operate today. *Lone Ranger, Lucy, Batman* and *The Man from UNCLE* may be expected, alas, only to urge backward viewers on to the blessedness which beckons, with the Gross National Product for ever rising, the electorate for ever voting, muzak for ever sounding and neon for ever shining.

The Problem of Pain

*A discussion with Archbishop Anthony Bloom
of the Russian Orthodox Church*

MUGGERIDGE: I suppose it would be true to say that in the modern world the tendency is to try and pretend that pain doesn't exist at all. I read once about a French king who thought that, if he was never confronted with the sight of a funeral, there would be no death, and I feel that somehow, by means of drugs and an attitude of mind, people try to pretend there's no such thing as pain. Do you agree with that?

BLOOM: Yes, I think there are two tendencies in the modern world which are equally wrong. The one is to pretend that things which do exist do not exist, because they are too painful to face; and the other one is, when they come your way because you cannot avoid it, simply to do away with them artificially. Pain-killers, tranquillizers, anything provided you do not face up to what is real.

MUGGERIDGE: Then, Archbishop, why is there pain in the universe? I think this is one of the greatest stumbling blocks today to people believing in religion at all. Why should there be this thing – pain?

BLOOM: Well, I think that you cannot answer that kind of question from the point of view of the believer while remaining on the ground of the unbeliever. One can argue about a system from within, and what those of us who believe in a personal God do believe is that the world, as we see it now, is not the world as God made and willed it. It is the free will of men that has introduced into it qualities, characteristics which do not belong to it originally. You may, of course, say – Why did God create man free? It would be so nice if nothing wrong had happened simply because nothing could happen. But then there would have been nothing good, either, because love, for instance, is conditioned by freedom. You may say that God has taken a risk, if you reason from man's point of view – the point of view of one who doesn't know the final outcome. But I would say God knew what He was doing, knew that it was worth the cost, and if you turn to certain saints they will answer the same – a man like St Seraphim of Sarov, who is a Russian saint who died in the middle of the nineteenth century, said that since he knew God he could say it was worth suffering, for thousands of years, every moment of one's life, in order to know Him.

MUGGERIDGE: To know that moment of ecstasy. Of course. Although not a particular believer myself, I feel that this is so. I think this horror of pain is a rather low instinct and that if I think of human beings I've known and of my own life, such as it is, I can't recall any case of pain which didn't, on the whole, enrich life.

BLOOM: I think it always does enrich life, and people who try to escape it from cowardice miss something extremely precious.

MUGGERIDGE: I think we ought also to take a concrete case. For instance, a person shrieking, howling in agony – the last stages of cancer, or something like that, or maybe an imbecile, a drooling imbecile. Along comes a materialist and says that such a life is now worth nothing, it should be painlessly ended. What about that?

BLOOM: Well, there is an old Russian saying that one should never take away what one cannot give back, and I think no human being is allowed to take life, because he cannot give it back, and he cannot even condition life.

MUGGERIDGE: So even as a doctor, which you were, you would say that it is never permissible to put out a life?

BLOOM: No, I think it is never permissible to put out a life.

MUGGERIDGE: And that the mere putting out of a life is a sin in all circumstances?

BLOOM: Yes, I think it's a wrong done to the person, which does not mean that you must not apply all your knowledge, all your skill, all your sympathy to make life more bearable and suffering less excruciating.

MUGGERIDGE: Of course, I wholly agree. I think that regarding human beings who are incapacitated as not entitled to live – which the Nazis embodied in legislation – is utterly horrible. But then let's take a borderline case. Let's imagine someone who is in great physical agony, and to ease the agony you must administer drugs. But by so doing you know as a doctor that you may very well be ending the patient's life. It could be so, I imagine?

BLOOM: Yes, it could.

MUGGERIDGE: How would you decide that dilemma?

BLOOM: I think you cannot impose on a man more than he can bear, and you can, you must bring him to the very edge of what is bearable. Yet you must do all you can to avoid his losing consciousness unnecessarily, which I think is done very often because people think that if a patient is unconscious he suffers less and his death will come in an easier way. This I think is wrong. But there is another thing which strikes me. In all these discussions (and this is implicit in your own question) there is an assumption that the person will not face up to pain. There is an assumption that every person is a coward, every person is incapable of rising to the level of great human courage. And this I think is unjust. I have met more than once people who seem to be the most ordinary kind of men and women, and who when confronted with tragedy were simply heroic.

And particularly, the case of a woman whom I had known very young, who happened to have a cancer of the breast, which was an acute cancer and developed within a very short time. She was a very simple believer, and she said, 'If God has sent me the suffering, there must be meaning in it, and there must also be strength in store for me.' And she refused to be helped by drugs. Up to the point when her chest was completely destroyed and one could see her lung breathing through the wound, until one day she woke and said, 'This night the Lord Christ has come close to me, and now it does not matter whether I suffer, or whether you help me out of it, because I have learned all I need learn from it.' And she accepted alleviation. She acted exactly to the contrary of what people usually do, or assume they would do.

MUGGERIDGE: That is very interesting. Of course, the Western church did oppose the use of anaesthetics, didn't it? Did the Eastern church do that too?

BLOOM: No, but I don't think it was for virtue's sake. It was simply ignorance, and partly, it didn't come into the scope of its activity.

MUGGERIDGE: Do you think there was any sense at all in that

opposition to the use of anaesthetics?

BLOOM: No, I don't think so. I think that a man should be offered every possibility there is to suffer less, but should also be taught and given courage to face up to much more than we usually do.

MUGGERIDGE: But you must have seen a large number of people die?

BLOOM: Yes, I have in fact.

MUGGERIDGE: We've lived through a lot of death in our time one way and another. And I imagine that people die very differently, I mean their mood when they die. Do you think that lots of people bitterly fear and dread death? Do you find that in your experience?

BLOOM: I think that Westerners seem to dread death much more than, say, the Russians. One of the things that impresses me in the Western attitude to death is that it is considered almost indecent to die. One should do that on the quiet. And when someone has died one hides him away, the children are not allowed to come and say a last goodbye to their parents or grandparents, and I find it shocking. What I find so often is that people should have been taught about death when they were full of sap and life, and when they could still face death not as a terror but as a challenge.

MUGGERIDGE: Of course, you see, Archbishop, death is the stranger at the feast of materialism and affluence. In America you know they make up corpses, they put lipstick on them, it is carried to the very limit; this pretence that it doesn't happen.

BLOOM: Yes exactly.

MUGGERIDGE: But I was thinking also of confronting the pain that goes with death. Do you find human beings predominantly cowardly or predominantly courageous?

BLOOM: I remember an admirable answer which was reported in the life of the French curé d'Ars concerning a sick child he was visiting; he said: 'Child, how can you bear your pain?' And the child smiled and said, 'Father, I have learnt to bear only the pain of the present moment. I don't feel any more yesterday's pain, nor yet tomorrow's.'

MUGGERIDGE: I think it applies also to happiness.

BLOOM: To everything.

MUGGERIDGE: I mean that the man who is thinking of tomorrow's happiness or yesterday's happiness is perhaps missing the whole idea of happiness.

BLOOM: Well, we miss everything when we cannot live in the present moment where the thing is real.

MUGGERIDGE: Yes, I'm sure that's right. I'm sure that's right. When people say how can there be a loving God, if the human race should be subjected to such tortures and miseries and destruction in so short a space of time, as we've seen, what do you say to people who say that?

BLOOM: Well there is a passage in the writing of the French theologian, John Danielou, that impressed me very greatly recently. He says something like: 'Suffering is the only meeting point between good and evil and the only chance for the evil one to be saved by the innocent.' And if you give more thought to it, you come to the conclusion that if good and evil never met, that is, if there was never suffering inflicted on the innocent by evil in general, or by an evil person in particular, there would be two parallel lines, the one of utter damnation, and the other one of salvation. But the law of life as we see it in nature, in human relationships, is that whenever one is evil someone who is innocent will suffer. One has drunk before he drove his car, and this child has been killed. I have been irresponsible before I performed an operation, and I have overlooked something of importance, and so on. This meeting point between the sufferer and the one who inflicts suffering is a point of crucial importance. It is the crossroads, it's also a cross, a real crucifixion at times. And the moment you suffer either great suffering or trivial suffering at the hand of someone and can forgive, you manifest really divine power.

MUGGERIDGE: You could apply that then to collective events. You could say the Nazis burnt up and killed six million Jews, the Stalinists killed three million peasants, and so on, and the fact of this, our wickedness resulting in this suffering, can purge the wickedness? Have I got that right?

BLOOM: Yes, I think I can give you an example, taken from a concentration camp, a prayer left on a sheet of wrapping paper, which in substance says: 'O Lord remember not only the men of goodwill but also the men of ill will. But do not remember all the suffering they have inflicted on us, remember the fruits we have gathered, thanks to this suffering – our comradeship, our loyalty, our humility, the courage, the generosity, the greatness of heart which has grown out of this, and when they come to judgement, let all the fruits which we have borne be their forgiveness.'

MUGGERIDGE: Therefore suffering is not a horrible thing necessarily? But a necessary thing, and sometimes an ennobling and elevating thing – is that right?

BLOOM: I think it is ennobling and I think it is creative, but it may be nonsense if you do not see meaning or put meaning into it. The mere fact of suffering does not make you a martyr.

Some little while ago I had a very edifying conversation on the telly about the problem of pain with a very distinguished and holy orthodox bishop, who like all orthodox bishops had a big black beard. And I thought we'd gone rather deeply into this subject. Imagine my surprise when the following day I got a taxi and the taxi driver said to me: 'I saw you yesterday with that bloke with a beard – you knocked hell out of him.' So don't worry, nobody's listening.

Lift up your Skirts

MUGGERIDGE: I've had my fair share of seeing the peculiar horrors that human eroticism can produce, and I regard *Playboy* as a particularly bad example, partly because it's hygienic and partly because it's more remote from the appetite that it's pandering to than any other version that I've seen. The thing about this particular animal side of man is that the further it gets from its true nature the more horrible it becomes. *Playboy* is a sort of processed, cellophane-wrapped, pasteurized, daisy-fresh, honeysweet sex. Well, sex isn't like that.

I had a session with Hugh Hefner in his house in Chicago. He was brought up a Methodist and has all the inhibitions and prejudices that go therewith. Now he's trying to persuade himself in what he calls the *Playboy* philosophy that you can have sex without tears. You know you used to have French without tears, as a way of learning French, but he says you may have sex without tears. Well of course you can't. Tears are an inseparable part of it. But he is the inspirer of an enormously successful enterprise. That in a materialist society puts you almost on to the level of a God. He has increased the gross national product. He's only increased it by a lot of erotic pictures and so on but still he's increased it, and millions of dollars have flowed in and all these people around Hefner are sycophantically disposed to him in exactly the same way as people were in an oriental court, because he is a success. I can't tell you what a strange atmosphere that house has. It's like something at the absolute heart of twentieth-century lunacy.

The Road to Canterbury

An Ursuline Nun's vocation

MUGGERIDGE: Of course from the point of view of the normal twentieth-century standards you've given up everything that people think makes life worthwhile.

SISTER MARY THOMAS: Yes, but you see, if I may say so I think this is typical of your attitude, Malcolm. You always look at the negative side of things. You don't see what I've gained. Take for instance the vow of chastity which of course intrigues everybody, this terrible thing that I've done, that I've given up –

MUGGERIDGE: I don't think that, incidentally –

SISTER MARY THOMAS: No – all right – but for me the vow of chastity has such a positive aspect as well as the negative; it's not just a question of what I've given up. You see, I have these natural instincts, womanly maternal instincts, which are thoroughly good in themselves, and which simply mustn't be stunted. I mustn't give them up. I must on the contrary develop them to the full, I must be a woman to the full, but I don't do this by developing them towards one person and one small family. If you like to put it in this way, I have this spiritual procreation with Christ through my union with Christ whose spouse I am. I bring forth children to Christ through union with Him in the spiritual way, and this is something more, much wider, much less exclusive and much more creative.

MUGGERIDGE: I think I can understand that. I mean personally of course. You're always hauling me over the coals for saying so, but I think that the things you've given up for the most part are not worth having.

SISTER MARY THOMAS: Yes, but you see, Malcolm, you've got to keep both feet on the ground all the same. You're living in this world.

MUGGERIDGE: Well that's an inescapable fact.

SISTER MARY THOMAS: Yes, but it seems to me that you're always trying to get too much out of this world.

MUGGERIDGE: I'm trying to look beyond it. Is that a wicked

thing to do?

SISTER MARY THOMAS: Well, I think you go too far; you see you don't seem to want the world at all. It seems to me you're like a shipwrecked man who finds himself in the water, and when he finds an opposition between the water and his body, he panics and fights and tries to get out of the water, to climb out of the water into the air. Well of course he can't do this, and so he drowns. But if he just changes his attitude he finds that this opposition will remain between the water and his body, but he can make it creative and he can float and make something creative out of the opposition, and he's saved.

Death on the Roads

The truth is that one of the most squalid and horrible things about the manner in which we live is our acceptance of this toll of life on the roads. I'm perfectly certain that future historians looking back will think that it was one of the most dreadful and callous things that's ever been, and I'm equally certain that it will not be stopped, or even prevented from increasing, until far more drastic action is taken. But if our cant about being a free society and regarding human life as the most precious thing meant anything at all we should do those drastic things.

Christianity and Politics

A conversation with Trevor Huddleston,
now Bishop of Masasi

MUGGERIDGE: 'Should a Christian keep out of politics?' is one of those very profound and important questions about which one doesn't naturally feel inclined to be dogmatic. Now we're going to take the particular case, at any rate to begin with, of Father Huddleston who is not only a Christian but a Christian priest. He wears the uniform of his church and, to some extent at any rate, his church is committed by what he does. And he felt bound – as probably most viewers know – in South Africa to take a certain very definite line politically, about apartheid. Now we're not discussing the goodness or badness of that. What we're discussing is whether someone like Father Huddleston, a Christian, a priest, is wise to identify himself with certain political movements and certain political activities whose end of course can't be foreseen, which might end in ways which would be very repugnant to him, but at the moment seem to him to represent goodness as against badness.

Now, Father Huddleston, I'm going to begin by the simplest possible question. Do you feel yourself that the action you took was right or wrong?

HUDDLESTON: I think I can honestly say I believe the action I took was right. I believe that I was caught in a particular situation in which human rights were involved, and of course it's very difficult to distinguish exactly between human rights and political rights.

MUGGERIDGE: Could you give us an example of action as distinct from a point of view?

HUDDLESTON: Yes, I think so. I was involved in trying to prevent the Government implementing the Western Areas Removal Scheme – a scheme which involved the uprooting of some seventy thousand Africans from their homes, expropriating their property, and placing them in a different locality. Now the

Government maintained that this was a slum clearance scheme. I maintained that it was part of the apartheid policy, in other words that the removal was not done from motives of bettering the African people but simply because it was in pursuance of a racial policy, and I felt and still feel that racialism is something wholly incompatible with the Christian faith. Therefore I felt bound by any means in my power, short of immoral ones, to oppose it.

MUGGERIDGE: But you did feel it right to identify yourself with action, with political action, taken in protest against that?

HUDDLESTON: Yes I most certainly did and looking back I still would feel that I could have done nothing else, and if I were in the same position tomorrow I would do the same thing.

MUGGERIDGE: I would like to ask you about a thing that's often puzzled me in relation to this whole problem. In the time, for instance, of St Paul there was the problem of slavery –

HUDDLESTON: Yes – certainly.

MUGGERIDGE: – and we all know that slavery is a vile thing, and various attempts were made to persuade St Paul to declare himself on that issue, which attempts, as I understand, he resisted.

In other words, what he did was to preach a gospel which of course in the end made slavery inconceivable, but he didn't identify himself with a movement – an immediate and local movement against slavery. Now wasn't he perhaps right in that?

HUDDLESTON: Well I think, of course, he was right, but there was no movement with which he could identify himself. But where St Paul speaks very clearly about slavery, as a matter of fact, is in the Epistle to Philemon, which is an epistle written to a slave owner about a Christian slave, and the whole foundation of that letter is, I think, one of the most moving and telling arguments against slavery in the whole Christian armour.

MUGGERIDGE: Without identifying himself with an anti-slavery movement?

HUDDLESTON: Yes, simply because there was no question of such a movement existing, but when the anti-slavery movement did come into existence in the time of Wilberforce in this country, Christians had to choose.

MUGGERIDGE: Well, that's my whole point – what St Paul had preached, as it were, came to fruition?

HUDDLESTON: Yes, but there were plenty of Christians who denied that there was any need whatsoever to argue for the abolition of slavery. In fact, if you read the debates in the House on that particularly subject –

MUGGERIDGE: There were Christians who failed –

HUDDLESTON: It was very much the Bishops, I'm afraid, who did argue very strongly that slavery was perfectly reasonable.

MUGGERIDGE: Now could I put another one. The Jews were subject people and the Romans were colonialists. Wasn't a tremendous pressure put on our Lord to identify Himself with that nationalist movement and didn't He resist it?

HUDDLESTON: Yes, you're perfectly correct I'm sure there. I mean, you've only got to think of Palm Sunday and the opportunity it would have given to our Lord to proclaim Himself the kind of King that the nationalists wanted. Nevertheless, you've got to remember that the Crucifixion was a political act, and our Lord, when He was questioned, as He was by Pilate, and when He was faced with this question – 'ART Thou a King then?' – didn't make any attempt whatsoever to explain His position away. If He had done Pilate could, and would no doubt, have released Him.

MUGGERIDGE: This terrific thing is not a new thing or a new dilemma for man, and in fact it arose in a very dramatic and immediate way during our Lord's life when He was asked, presumably by some cunning person who wanted to trip Him up, 'Should we give tribute to Caesar' – and He made the marvellous answer 'Render unto Caesar the things that are Caesar's and unto God the things that are God's'. Like all wonderful answers it doesn't really answer. Father Huddleston, would you agree that is the absolute nub of the thing?

HUDDLESTON: I would say this, that our Lord deliberately gave an equivocal answer because as He looked forward through the centuries He saw that at certain times in history it would be most necessary to render unto God the things that are God's, and therefore the emphasis there is more on how we are to be quite certain that we are rendering to God the things that are God's. Surely what is absolutely vital in society is that man, created in the image and likeness of God, should be able to find and fulfil himself as a person. In other words, that the state is made for man and not man for the state, and therefore, if the church is to be true to her vocation she's got to go on insisting that certain things belong to God and nobody else.

Air Travel

In an aeroplane one senses the fallacy of travel. The faster and higher they go, the more they seem to stand still.

The Pattern of Society in 2000 A.D.

Questioned by John Tusa

TUSA: Mr Muggeridge, do you think that by the year 2000 there'll be less social inequality than there is now?

MUGGERIDGE: I should expect there to be more because the present trend is towards more. Everywhere that you look, for instance, whether it's Communist countries or highly-developed capitalist countries, inequality is on the increase. It's only curiously enough in the very old-fashioned snobbish countries like this one where any brake is put on this process. Contrary to the generally-held view, snobbishness is a brake on inequality. It doesn't mean that snobbishness is good necessarily, but it has that effect.

TUSA: You even say this about Communist countries – about Soviet Russia?

MUGGERIDGE: Oh, I'm sure of it. The difference between someone who is in the 'apparat' there and someone who is not is greater than in any society that I've ever been in. In terms of amenities, of what they can do, of what they have, of the freedom they enjoy.

TUSA: So you think that material development in the countries in the West won't narrow down material inequality. Take the United States?

MUGGERIDGE: On the contrary, because I think the rich are getting even richer and more important in the United States and the difference between the ordinary humdrum man and the successful man is getting bigger and bigger.

TUSA: Well, what sort of people do you think will run society? What sort of people are going to be at the top of this society?

MUGGERIDGE: I think the operators are going to be at the top – the people who can work this extraordinary apparatus of mass communications. We see that to some extent now. The sort of man who's emerging to power in all the countries of the world, the important countries of the world, is the sort of – again to use the Russian word – 'apparatchik'. Now, in Russia Khrush-chev has gone, and the two men who've taken his place are anonymous men really. And I think also in America.

TUSA: But what about the place of the person who is very intelligent, very highly educated – what people call the merito-cracy? Won't they be at the top?

MUGGERIDGE: No. That man has either got to reconcile himself to serving the apparatus or to being subversive, a rebel, an out-sider. This is exactly how it's working out.

TUSA: Now then, these operators, they'll be at the top. What will the status symbols of these people be? Will they be money and possessions as they seem to be now?

MUGGERIDGE: I don't think so. I think the trend is all against that. It's an old-fashioned idea of power giving you, for in-stance, great possessions – a big house, marvellous uniforms, a possibility of indulging yourself, whether it be women or what-ever it may be. That's very largely past and the pursuit now is power for its own sake. If you look around the world at the people who are running it, you don't find those flamboyant characters. You find these men who derive, for some mysterious reason, enormous satisfaction out of just possessing power.

TUSA: So the leaders of the year 2000 will almost be personally austere men?

MUGGERIDGE: I would expect them to be so. Because I don't think that self-indulgent men could stand the strain.

TUSA: Well, this I think leads us on possibly to the question of religion. Do you see any future for organized religion by the year 2000?

MUGGERIDGE: Of course, I have to speak about the Christian religion because we live in a Christian part of the world. It might conceivably be different in Buddhist parts, but I think it's roughly the same. I regret to say that I think that our religion, our Christian religion, in its organized sense is over. It's coming to an end. In Communist régimes and near-Communist régimes it is deliberately destroyed because it conflicts with any form of collectivist society. In the successful capitalist countries like America and to some extent this country, it's not destroyed – it's not wiped out – but it's taken over, it's integrated into a materialist view of life and a materialist society, and in being so integrated, of course, it's destroyed.

TUSA: What will survive? Will it be a personal form of Christianity?

MUGGERIDGE: I think it's possible, and this is where I would be a tiny bit hopeful. I think it's possible it might survive as a sort of underground, a sort of subversive movement. It began, you know, in catacombs. It began as an underground, illicit movement; it might revert to that.

TUSA: And you think then it'll be fighting against a more or less unrelieved materialism in society?

MUGGERIDGE: Yes, but it would have some very powerful cards in its hand. The fact is, of course, that materialist society is excessively boring. What brings it down is not really its brutality but its emptiness. And of course this creates a mood in which people will be highly susceptible to the appeal of a religion like Christianity. This is noticeable in the Communist countries. One of the undoubted miracles of our time is the survival of Christianity in these countries, and as you see, in a writer like Pasternak, not only its survival but its captivation of some of the highest intelligences. Now, this is a remarkable fact and this could happen of course.

TUSA: I wonder whether this question of boredom with the material will affect sexual behaviour. I mean, do you expect sexual behaviour to be relatively restrained or will it be completely free? Will people be able to do what they wish?

MUGGERIDGE: I think we're headed absolutely directly for a sort of broiler-house system. A system in which appetite as such is everything. But of course that won't work because there is something in human beings that wishes to translate this appetite into terms of a permanent human relationship. Otherwise the institute of matrimony would not have gone on. I'm sure you would agree with me the odds are heavily against it.

TUSA: And you think that this too will defeat itself just by being too easy, too boring?

MUGGERIDGE: Too boring and ultimately destructive even of appetite, even of sexual desire.

TUSA: Will this society in the year 2000 be more or less cruel? Come to that, how cruel do you think society is now?

MUGGERIDGE: Well, I think that the fifty years of my conscious life have been the most cruel and brutal half-century in all history. Of course, I quite realize that in certain respects –

economic relations and so on in the developed countries – there is a greater humanity. But by and large the actual volume of cruelty in my time in these highly civilized countries – countries which devote an enormous amount of money and effort to things like education – cruelty has exceeded that of any comparable period and not only cruelty but callousness.

TUSA: And will this be worse?

MUGGERIDGE: I think there's every indication that it'll go on.

TUSA: Well, bearing all this in mind, do you think that you'd like to be alive in the year 2000?

MUGGERIDGE: Let me say that I do not take the view that life is different at different times; it's circumstances that are different. But the experience of living seems to me to be approximately the same. That is why if I read Homer, if I read Shakespeare, if I read Dr Johnson, if I read the contemporary writers, I'm reading about the same thing – I'm reading about life, although the actual circumstances of life for those people are completely different. Therefore, I think in 2000 life will be approximately – the experience of living will be approximately – as now; and it would make no difference whether I lived then or now. I would have the possibility of understanding as I have now, and the possibility of failing to understand.

Humour

Bad humour is an evasion of reality; good humour is an acceptance of it.

McMothballs

I would have said that Mr Macmillan had a tiny tiny flavour of mothballs about him.

A Hard Bed to Lie On

*A visit to the Cistercian monks of Nunraw
in Scotland. They received a special dispensation to
break their rule of silence for this programme*

It's half past three in the morning when, for Cistercian monks,
the day begins with private devotions and then the Mass. I, too,
attend the Mass, kneeling at the back; an outsider. To me it
means nothing beyond the spectacle of devout men, the pleasant
sound of plainsong. To the monks it is everything – the pivot of
their lives, a daily spiritual feast compensating them for the
austerities and privations of their strict Cistercian Rule. Are
they wasting their time? There are many today who think so.
Prayers don't show in the Gross National Product – so why
pray? The monks have an answer: the Mass brings them, they
say, spiritual nourishment – the body and blood of Christ to
swallow ravenously.

Could I ever have been a monk, I ask myself. I can see the
attraction of the life – dying in the flesh to be reborn in the
spirit. Marvellous! No newspapers, no telly – what joy! But
living in a dormitory – communal life and all the little irrita-
tions and peculiarities it generates! That I should find tough.
Young men still come forward to take it on. Will there be
enough of them to fill the large new Abbey high up on a hill
which the monks have built to move to from their present old
army huts and Victorian mansion?

At meals the Cistercian rule of silence applies at its strictest.
The food is still plain and monotonous, but not as meagre as it
once was. Nowadays, the monks have cheese, but still no meat
or fish or eggs. It all somehow reminds me a little of army life –
with the refectory a kind of holy, silent NAAFI.

After Mass and breakfast – in the fields. The monks farm a
thousand and more acres, and pride themselves on being good
farmers. After all, they've been at it for some ten centuries. It's
part of their rule thus to provide by their own labour for their
own needs; not to be a burden on others. Yet some of the

younger monks feel that their old-fashioned farming is too remote from today's technological world. They'd sooner work in
factories. The twentieth century with all its unresolved doubts
and conflicts has somehow penetrated this enclosed order. The
Bishop of Woolwich, as it were, has got into the woodwork;
Teillard de Chardin, Paul Tillich are scuttling about under the
floorboards. The older monks stick to their rule and Thomas
Aquinas.

The new Abbey is nearly finished. It's on any showing an heroic
effort, the culmination of twenty years of effort and work by the
monks. The design by Peter Whiston is based on Citeau where
St Bernard's great Ministry began. How proud he would have
been to know that after a thousand years yet another Abbey
would be built and occupied in a distant land. Next year the
monks will move in – a great day for all of them but also not
without its questionings.

MUGGERIDGE: You look very young, Brother Martin. How long
have you been a monk?
MARTIN: I've been here about six and a half years.
MUGGERIDGE: So you can take your solemn vows quite soon.
MARTIN: I've taken my solemn vows.
MUGGERIDGE: I see, but not your lifelong vows.
MARTIN: Yes, solemn vows are lifelong vows. Simple profes-
sion is just temporary vows.
MUGGERIDGE: So you are a Cistercian monk for life. Presum-
ably you have deliberated long and weighed the matter up and
prayed over it and so on?
MARTIN: Well, that's an odd question, because I think for some
men they do have a lot of thinking to do and questions to ask,
but I found with myself that once I had decided to go on, long
before the six months' probationary period was up, I had no
more worries at all.
MUGGERIDGE: Marvellous!
MARTIN: That was my experience, not others'.
MUGGERIDGE: It's a difficult life, Brother Martin, isn't it?
MARTIN: Spartan. I suppose that some of the things that we put
up with might put other people off; the monotonous round that
we have, the very simple food we have; the fact that we never,

or rarely, get out anywhere. Other people can always go to the cinema or the theatre . . .

MUGGERIDGE: But you can't.

MARTIN: We don't have anything like that, no.

MUGGERIDGE: Each day is like the one before.

MARTIN: And so much so that one doesn't always know what day it is.

MUGGERIDGE: You don't read daily newspapers?

MARTIN: No.

MUGGERIDGE: I should regard that as one of the great benefits of being a monk. That is one of the things that would attract me most. But there's a movement for having newspapers, isn't there?

MARTIN: A lot of us feel that our lack of political knowledge is a hindrance to possibly living this life as we want to live it.

MUGGERIDGE: Would that be a difference between you younger monks and the older ones?

MARTIN: Well, that's hard to say. It may just be a sign of one's youthfulness. I don't know what I will think about it in ten years' time.

MUGGERIDGE: Is there a rift, Brother Martin, of any kind between the younger monks and the older monks? I mean a different attitude towards your way of life?

MARTIN: Well now, sometimes I think there is and sometimes I don't think there is. I certainly feel that the pressures of modern life give us a different outlook on the Cistercian life.

MUGGERIDGE: Different, you mean, from the older monks?

MARTIN: I think so, yes. And it takes time for us to appreciate their viewpoint. What may well change is that we have been up to now – and still are in this monastery – predominantly an agricultural organization. Our history is wrapped up in agriculture through the centuries. But it may be that monks may think in the future that they ought to move away from the agricultural world into a closer relationship with the people in the cities.

MUGGERIDGE: How long have you been a monk, Brother Oliver?

OLIVER: Well, I entered Rosscrae in 1934, that's in Rosscrae, of course, in Tipperary, and I was there up until I came to Scotland in 1946.

MUGGERIDGE: When you are doing all this outdoor work on the farm, aren't you sometimes hungry?

OLIVER: Yes, you sometimes come home tired. And although the bed is a hard one, you know the old saying that the Cistercian bed is hard to lie on, but it's sweet to die on.

MUGGERIDGE: And you found it a bed hard to lie on?

OLIVER: Oh, indeed I always have done, and to this day I do. That's the one consolation you get when you go to a hospital – you get a lovely soft bed. You can sleep and sleep, and the last time I was in hospital the sister there said she thought I was never going to waken. She said I slept for six days without break – so there you are. That is a fact!

MUGGERIDGE: But sweet to die on?

OLIVER: Yes, it is sweet to die on. Well, that's the reward of a monk's life. I suppose he comes into the monastery to die, or to learn how to die perhaps.

MUGGERIDGE: Is that what you see as the purpose of living in a monastery – to learn how to die?

OLIVER: I think it is – now that's my purpose. I don't say it's everybody's perhaps, but if I didn't think I was going to get to heaven I wouldn't be here three days!

MUGGERIDGE: Why the Cistercians, Father Hugh?

HUGH: Because of the balance of the life. As you have seen, our life is spread out between three activities, divine office and choir, the reading or *Lexio Divina*, and the manual work. It gives a balanced day and a balanced background for a life of prayer.

MUGGERIDGE: As I understand, a lot of changes have either happened or are pending in the Cistercian rule. Do you think all this is in the right direction?

HUGH: If a living being cannot adapt itself to different conditions, the new conditions will overwhelm it and will die. We must be men of our day. For instance, I don't think fasting plays quite the same part as it did in a former era. I would say that the pain in the neck today is for the old to put up with the young and the young to put up with the old.

MUGGERIDGE: You mean that would be the real mortification of the flesh?

HUGH: I would say the real mortification of the flesh is the brush of temperament in a life like ours. I don't think it's the physical austerity, I don't think it's the hard beds. You can get used to that. But things like the brush of temperament is something very much harder.

MUGGERIDGE: When you say the brush of temperament, what you mean is people, monks getting on each other's nerves in the nearness of their lives. Is that right?

HUGH: Well, what I mean is things like having a monk next to you in choir who sings habitually flat. It can be very trying, you see. We wouldn't have you in.

MUGGERIDGE: No, I'm sure you wouldn't. I wouldn't even apply to sing in your choir, because I listen to you holding forth like – a singing bird.

It's half past seven in the evening. For the monks it's the end of another day; their work's over, with only the last office, Compline – to me the loveliest of all – to be sung, then bed. So their days pass, in prayer, work and study; each exactly like the other, the weeks and the months and the years passing and taking them, as the older monks like Brother Oliver confidently believe, nearer to Heaven, or as the younger ones ardently hope, along some path of special illumination.

Will there be enough new vocations to make up their numbers? It's asking a tremendous lot in this age of affluence and materialsm to ask a young man to accept this austere disciplined way of life. Whatever may happen to the Cistercians, to the church, or even to Christianity itself, I'm quite sure of one thing: there'll always be a demand among human beings for some to withdraw from the pursuit of fame and money and power and sexual satisfaction and all these other things to which men dedicate their lives, and seek some special relationship with their Creator. And that's what the monks here have tried to do, and the efforts they've made won't be lost.